THE ALLURE OF GRAMMAR

UNDER DISCUSSION
Marilyn Hacker and Kazim Ali, General Editors
Donald Hall, Founding Editor

Volumes in the Under Discussion series collect reviews and essays about individual poets. The series is concerned with contemporary American and English poets about whom the consensus has not yet been formed and the final vote has not been taken. Titles in the series include:

The Allure of Grammar

The Glamour of Angie Estes's Poetry

Doug Rutledge, Editor

UNIVERSITY OF MICHIGAN PRESS

Ann Arbor

Published in the United States of America by the
University of Michigan Press
Printed and bound by CPI Group (UK) Ltd, Croydon, CR0 4YY
First published March 2019

A CIP catalog record for this book is available from the British Library.

Library of Congress Cataloging-in-Publication Data

Library of Congress Cataloging-in-Publication Data

Names: Rutledge, Douglas F., 1951- editor.
Title: The allure of grammar : the glamour of Angie Estes's poetry / Doug
    Rutledge, editor.
Description: Ann Arbor : University of Michigan Press, 2019. | Series: Under
    discussion | Includes bibliographical references. |
Identifiers: LCCN 2018053133 (print) | LCCN 2018059198 (ebook) | ISBN
    9780472125067 (E-book) | ISBN 9780472037377 (pbk. : alk. paper)
Subjects: LCSH: Estes, Angie--Criticism and interpretation.
Classification: LCC PS3555.S76 (ebook) | LCC PS3555.S76 Z54 2019 (print) |
    DDC 811/.6--dc23
LC record available at https://lccn.loc.gov/2018053133

Acknowledgments

Grateful acknowledgment is given to the following publishers to reprint previously published material:

The poetry of Angie Estes appears courtesy of Oberlin College Press.

Julianne Buchsbaum, "Beyond Lyric: Review of *Voice-Over*." *Slope* 20, Summer 2004.

Kevin Clark, "The Chapbook as Optic Lens." This is a section of "The Chapbook as Optic Lens" that appeared in *Negative Capability*, Spring 1992. Reprinted by permission of the author and publisher.

Langdon Hammer, "The Voice Is Ready to Sing: A Review of *Enchantée*." *The American Scholar*, September 4, 2012. Reprinted by permission of the author and publisher.

Nancy Kuhl, "On Angie Estes's *Chez Nous*." *Laurel Review*, Winter 2006. Reprinted by permission of the author and publisher.

Karen Rigby, "Means of Transport, Medieval Mind: A Dialogue with Angie Estes." *Cerise Press* 1.3, Spring 2010. Reprinted by permission of the author and publisher.

Doug Rutledge, "Triste Trystes." A shorter version of this essay originally appeared as "Review of Angie Estes's *Tryst*." *The Journal* 34.1, Spring/Summer 2010. Reprinted by permission of the author and publisher.

Doug Rutledge, "'*Visibile Parlare*': Ekphrastic Images in the Poetry of Angie Estes." In *Ekphrasis in American Poetry: The Colonial Period to the 21st Century*, ed. Sandra Kleppe. Newcastle,

UK: Cambridge Scholars Press, 2015. Reprinted by permission of the author and publisher.

Christopher Spaide, "Ready to Sing: Angie Estes's *Enchantée*." *Los Angeles Review of Books*, May 22, 2015. Reprinted by permission of the author and publisher.

Many thanks to Susan Cronin, Marcia LaBrenz and the editorial staff at the University of Michigan Press. Thanks also to David Walker, David Young, and the staff at Oberlin College Press. Finally, deep gratitude to Rebecca, without whose support and understanding this book would not have been possible.

Contents

Digital materials related to this title can be found on the Fulcrum platform via the following citable URL: https://doi.org/10.3998/mpub.9962940

DOUG RUTLEDGE

Introduction

In Angie Estes's poem "*Lieu De Moxie Mémoire*," the speaker blesses
"the official in the Musée d'Orsay / who gave me the green sticker
to wear: *Droit / de Parole*."[1] Certainly, after six books of poetry,
Estes has exercised her right to speak poetically. Through the pro-
cess of winning the prestigious Kingsley Tufts Award, a Guggen-
heim, the Alice Fay di Castagnola Prize from the Poetry Society of
America, a Pushcart Prize, being one of two finalists for the Pulitzer
Prize, and achieving a long list of other accolades, Estes's poetic
speech is admired by other poets as well as a growing and dedicated
audience. Nevertheless, for this poet, who has said she distrusts nar-
rative, there remains a question about how best to approach her
poetry. Estes employs cultural objects and what she refers to as "di-
vine details" (see the interview with Karen Rigby starting on pg.
67) in the fashion similar to that of an imagist poet, and critics have
pointed out that her work is a linguistic tour de force. Those con-
cepts will be explored in the coming pages; for now, however, I
would like to begin by approaching her poetry through the very
traditional concepts of sound and sense.

Stephanie Burt asserts that "Angie Estes has recently created
some of the most beautiful verbal objects on the planet."[2] It takes
little effort to find examples of the beauty Burt describes: "But the
moon has not one / iota of *I ought to*, even with its waxing tab / of
IOUs,"[3] "*Lieu De Moxie Mémoire*" continues. The playful inner line
rhymes and the repeated "ou" sounds are engaging. Indeed, the
poet is referring to one of Debussy's most lovely compositions
through the folk song to which she alludes. But even here Estes is
not being as frivolous as her play with sound might lead us to be-
lieve, for she tells us that she is "off / to Arezzo to jot a note, the way
Pierrot / called out to the moon . . ."[4] repeating the importance of
writing. In "Au Clair de la Lune" (By the Light of the Moon), Pier-
rot, a comic character, is being called upon by a neighbor for the
loan of a pen, so the neighbor might write a word. As well as refer-
ring to the immediate need to write, this folk song and children's

lullaby is full of double entendre, expressing the religious experience and the light of God. Indeed, *pour l'amour de Dieu* is a repeated refrain, so the poem seems about both the need to write and the need to have a spiritual experience.

Similarly, Estes's poem recounts the mounds of joy marking the stops royal funerals made to pray on the way to Saint Denis, the cathedral where the bodies would be buried. The poem also recalls the "*Vierge Ouvrante* statue of the nursing Virgin / that opens to reveal God holding Christ / on the cross."[5] At the poem's conclusion, the speaker asks, "in accordance with the laws / of perspective, arrest me."[6] Because the poet mentions Piero Francesca, an Italian Renaissance painter, the word perspective, if taken literally, would refer to the way artists make a two-dimensional space appear three-dimensional. However, because the poet has asked us to consider life and death as well as outer space metaphorically, the word assumes a spiritual as well as a spatial dimension. As for the last phrase, "arrest me," I am reminded of John Donne's Holy Sonnet XIV: "imprison mee for I, / Except you enthrall me never shall be free, / Nor ever chast, except you ravish mee."[7]

In another poem, of which I am particularly fond, "Wrap in Parchment and Pink Paper," we find a different way in which the beauty of Estes's lines leads to an understanding of her poetry. The penultimate stanza of the poem begins:

> the part that's in love with
> God dissolves into *Cheap Rose Hip*
> *Kisses: with the small spoon*
> *make kisses on oblaten paper*
> *and bake in a low oven.*[8]

The lovely alliteration of "s's" here recreates the sound for the alert reader of sipping rose-hip tea. The rhythm of these lines almost lulls us to sleep, as the tea might, until we reach the last line of the stanza: "What could be / carried across Terezín was a recipe. . . ."[9] The "z" in Terezín gives us a kind of "s" sound, too, but one that is slightly altered. Rather than making us sleepy, it alerts the reader to a change of mood. Terezín Ghetto was a concentration camp. The Nazis presented it as an ideal Jewish settlement. However, more than thirty-three thousand people died there of malnutrition and disease.

Earlier in the poem, the speaker describes an ancient funerary ritual in which "the dead were / placed in the fetal position, waiting

/ to unfold again, tongues held // like viatica in the mouth."[10] Viatica is, of course, the Eucharist. The poet then establishes a parallel image of the women in the ghetto:

> What can be
> translated into heaven, *should be high*
> *& beautiful.* Because Mina Pächter
> and the women of Terezín could not
> be transported out of the ghetto
> in which they starved, they talked
>
> and even argued about the correct way
> to prepare food they might never eat
> again—*cooking with the mouth*,
> they called it. . . .[11]

By echoing "Viatica in the mouth" with "cooking with the mouth," Estes seems to imply an equivalence between taking the Eucharist and imprisoned Jewish women engaging in imaginary, or more precisely, remembered cooking. This is a profound and moving metaphorical leap.

In order to think about why Estes is asking us to compare "cooking with the mouth" with the Eucharist, and also to think about the larger question about how Estes writes and therefore how we should read her poetry, allow me to take a short side trip through the history of poetry. Stephanie Burt has referred to Estes's poetry as "nearly Baroque."[12] Many English poets of the Baroque period, the late sixteenth and seventeenth centuries, have come to be called metaphysical, a term coined by Dr. Samuel Johnson, writing in the age of reason, who famously said of them:

> But wit, abstracted from its affects upon the hearer, may be more rigorously and philosophically considered as a kind of *discordia concors*; a combination of dissimilar images or discovery of occult resemblances in things apparently unlike. . . . The most heterogeneous ideas are yoked by violence together.[13]

Dr. Johnson did not like this yoking, but in the twentieth and twenty-first centuries, we have enjoyed a renewed appreciation of the metaphysical poets, John Donne being perhaps the best-known example.

In the "Canonization," the unlike things Donne yokes together are secular and divine love, though he gives us several other examples of *discordia concors* in the process:

Call us what you will, wee are made such by love;
Call her one, mee another flye,
We'are tapers too, and at our owne cost die,
And wee in us finde the Eagle and the Dove.
The phoenix ridle hath more wit
    By us; we two, being one, are it.
So, to one neutrall thing both sexes fit.
    Wee die and rise the same and prove
    Mysterious by this love.

Wee can dye by it, if not live by love,
    And if unfit for tombs and hearse
Our legend bee, it will be fit for verse;
    And if no peece of Chronical wee prove,
    We'll build in sonnets pretty roomes;
    As well a well wrought urne becomes
The greatest ashes, as halfe-acre tombes,
    And by these hymnes, all shall approve
    Us *Canoniz'd* for love.[14]

Comparing flies and candles to people is strange enough. However, as the title suggests, the primary group of unlike things compared in the poem are secular lovers with saints who have been canonized. Another lovely level is the comparison between sonnets and the urns, so the poem itself becomes a ritualistic container, which serves as a reliquary and holds the remains of the sainted lovers. Finally, the process of sanctification occurs as the lovers become flies or candles, dying to be reborn like the phoenix. Left unstated, of course, is the Renaissance belief that making love was itself a kind of death that could lead to new life.

This is a narrative poem only by the slimmest of margins. True, it is a dramatic monologue in which a speaker is declaiming to an imaginary listener, but the rhetoric only makes a limited amount of sense as a story. It is primarily interpretable as we compare the images to a pattern made clear by the title.

Estes also brings together a series of images, which at first don't always seem similar. However, they do operate in a metaphorical manner, and realizing this makes the joy of the music become vivified with the poem's meaning. Returning to "Wrap in Parchment and Also Pink Paper," I would like to suggest that this poem is operating like Donne's "Canonization," not only in the way it employs images but also in the goal of those images. When Estes compares "viatica in the mouth," to "cooking with the mouth," she has begun to sanctify these starving women who love through cooking, even when they have no food, saying they

> wrote their recipes
> on whatever scraps of paper
> they could find: *like strudel, fill*
>
> *as desired. One can do everything*
> *with* the body, *fill to your*
> *liking,* but only what's legible
> remains—like the bones
> of saints disinterred and
> translated into reliquaries. . . .[15]

Here Estes is again comparing unlike things: Jewish prisoners to Christian saints. But clearly the poet is making a larger point about suffering and love through suffering transforming a human being into something holy, in fact, so holy that human limitations of sect or religion cannot put a boundary on the holiness they have achieved.

"Wrap in Parchment and Also Pink Paper" indicates another tendency in Estes's work, which is that her poetry often weaves together the ordinary (in this case the less than ordinary) with the mysterious or the sublime. Almost always in an Estes poem, some everyday experience is blended with something extraordinary. The extraordinary could be as simple as the italic font, or as sophisticated as ballet or a medieval cathedral, but there is consistently something in an Estes poem to raise readers above their normal experiences, so that daily emotion or routine activities are made to resonate with high works of art or important cultural artifacts. In this way, Estes consistently weaves immediate felt responses into a larger, emotionally significant cultural fabric. Consequently, Estes's poetry is often uplifting, though, as "Wrap in Parchment and Also Pink Paper" suggests, the tonal landscape of her poetry remains complex.

As we noted earlier, Angie Estes employs art and "divine details" in her poetry, in the fashion of imagist poets, a title referring to a modernist group of poets, including Ezra Pound and Marianne Moore. T. S. Eliot is also often associated with this group. When Estes employs a series of images in a poem, she often wishes them to be compared with each other metaphorically. This is part of what Estes means when, in an interview reprinted in this volume, she says that she has been doing a kind of medieval thinking most of her life:

"reading the details of this world in the light of some other world." However, that crescendo of metaphorical comparisons also operates emotionally and builds up to a moving (cathartic) climax. This is why T. S. Eliot offers the following advice to a poet, whose work he is rejecting for publication in a journal he was editing:

> What I think is that it is too thoughtful. That is to say, the harder you think and the longer you think the better: but in turning thought into poetry it has to be fused into a more definite pattern of immediately apprehensible imagery, imagery which shall have its own validity and be immediately the equivalent of, and indeed be identical with, the thought behind it. A great many very good poems just miss reaching this point. The result is something which we have to *think* instead of immediately apprehending. The more thought that is turned into poetry the better; only it must be, in the final form, *felt* thought.[16]

Angie Estes has mastered the ability to create felt thought by building a series of images that increase in emotional intensity, while at the same time building a thematic coherence, which is achieved as the reader is asked to compare one image to the next. This is why she is admired by so many poets.

The book that follows this introduction is primarily written by poets, who are examining the way Estes makes her poetry beautiful and meaningful in order to improve their own work as well as to show their students how to write better poetry. These poets focus on the manner in which Estes crafts language and the way that language creates an emotional response as well as meaning within the structured environment of the poem, or as Estes herself puts it, the way "the poem [becomes] an arranged place . . . where experience happens." Therefore, in an important way, this is a craft book, a book about looking at the way fine poetry works. It is also a teaching tool, a way to bring both good poetry and understanding of that poetry into the creative writing and literature classroom. Finally, it is an introduction to and an examination of the work of one of America's finest living poets.

The sheer joy one can derive from reading her poetry is the subject of David Young's essay, "Angie Estes: Five Pleasures." Young brings a poet's ear to Estes's work when he describes the "pleasure in language" one derives from her poetry. Young is focused on assisting a reader new to Estes's work or perhaps new to poetry itself.

Therefore, when he moves on to the "pleasures in languages (plural)," he points out that the poet herself guides us through her use of foreign words, so readers enjoy new discoveries in her work, rather than being intimidated by the unfamiliar. Young goes on to share with us the pleasures in history, juxtaposition, and music he takes in Estes's poetry.

Julianne Buchsbaum considers the way those pleasures add to meaning and to self-discovery. In her review of *Voice-Over*, Buchsbaum asserts that Estes's poems "reveal a place in language where past and present, meaning and music converge." She argues that the poetic voice is trying to discover itself, in some sense the speaker's true home by navigating through art, music, and language.

In "Memory, Grief, and the Linguistic Artifact in Angie Estes's Poems," Leah Falk approaches Estes's poetry from the point of view of a poet who is constantly interested in improving her craft. Falk, a former student of Estes's, describes writing prompts the older poet would assign as insight into the way Estes writes. Falk explains that Estes "relies on the idea that the bodies of words are not coincidental, but rather the results of our human process of collecting, recording and forgetting. They are tiny arguments about the procedures of history." In Falk's reading, Estes's poems create environments in which "a single word can transpose reality, or provide a clue to another consciousness." So in Estes's poetic world, synonyms, puns and linguistic errors reveal meaning not only in the images and events the poem explores but in the human history revealed in the complex and contradictory process of attaching meaning to words.

In "A Lawless Proposition: Angie Estes and the Line," Ahren Warner declares that as a teacher of creative writing he is most often drawn to employing Estes's poetry as an example of the way a poet can use line-breaks to evoke a multitude of meanings, meanings that often contradict each other. Indeed, the implication of Estes's line-breaks often seems to be both true and not true. This means that the reader has to become an active participant in the production of the poem itself. According to Warner, Estes's line-breaks undermine the unity of the lyric "I." Finally, he argues that Estes's poetry is a form of thought that can only be expressed as poetry.

How Estes approaches this visual effect of her poetry is the concern of Lee Upton in her essay "On Angie Estes: An Erotics of Italics." Upton offers a series of important insights about both the writing and the reading of Estes's poetry. She notes the close focus Estes has on the materials of her art, even something as apparently trivial as the alphabet. According to Upton, the decorative is often associated with women and considered to be trivial, but to Estes it is life-affirming. For Estes, Upton points out, a font such as italics serves as "an enhancement of pleasure." Italics speak for what is off stage, strangely for what is both absent and present in the poem, for what is lost but still remembered. Italics even mark "intractable contrasts in power. The visual imprints of italics," Upton concludes, "contribute to the way Estes's poems constellate meaning and summon beauty."

Estes's third book was reviewed by Nancy Kuhl, who tells us that "throughout *Chez Nous* Estes is interested in the way language maps both interior and exterior landscapes, exposing contours and corners, pathways and distances." Kuhl points out that Estes writes poetry by piling image upon image. Her linguistic precision, Kuhl argues, coupled with the ambiguity of language itself, implies that it might be impossible to write poetry in any other way. Kuhl concludes that Estes is constantly interested in the way poetic language transforms us.

Estes speaks about her sense of the poetic and the way comparisons work in her thinking and in her poetry in "Means of Transport, Medieval Mind: Dialogue with Angie Estes." It is worth pointing out that this dialogue is not simply the result of an hour's discussion. It took months to create with interviewer Karen Rigby writing back and forth with the poet. Therefore, the interview is a carefully thought-out exploration of Estes's aesthetic. Here the poet explains that she has always been practicing a kind of medieval thinking, which she defines as an intellectual environment where experiences and objects in one world suggest something profound about the next. She reveals that she thinks of a poem as a place arranged with what she calls "divine details," where experience happens. Importantly, Estes makes a point of saying that this arrangement is not narrative. She claims that this way of thinking about poetry reaches back from Wallace Stevens and Emily Dickinson through a long lineage of poets. "I believe," she continues, "that a work of art—or a poem—must make an arrangement that creates an experience for a viewer or reader, that pulls the reader into the work of art, so that something happens to the viewer."

Something indeed happens to the reader in *Enchantée,* Estes's fifth book, according to Langdon Hammer. Hammer concludes that "Estes breaks language apart to see how it might be reconfigured. She pursues not sound over sense but the sense that sound itself makes. . . ." This combination of sound and sense, he argues, transports the reader.

In "Wonderlust: Angie Estes's Spiral Aesthetic," Jill Allyn Rosser, another poet, examines Estes's fascination with language. Rosser asserts that Estes cares for her instrument, language, the way a violinist might care for a Stradivarius. However, Rosser adds another interesting dimension when she suggests that as the poet jumps from image to image she sometimes seems to be engaging in what a psychologist might call an avoidance procedure, an insight that leads us to ask about the painful emotions or events the poet is both alluding to and trying to ignore.

In "The Chapbook as Optic Lens," a review of Estes's *Boarding Pass*, her earliest collection, Kevin Clark also considers the occasionally painful combination of the poetic and the personal. Clark sees these early poems as a lens through which the poet observes and perhaps struggles to rearrange the often-contradictory images and experiences that challenge her identity. According to Clark, the primary difficulty the poet faces is a culture unwilling to accept a lesbian lifestyle. However, Clark does not limit the chapbook's strength to the political. Indeed, he celebrates its depth.

I also consider personal themes in my review of *Tryst*. I am especially interested in the pun Estes plays with triste trysts, that is, sad meetings. In the first poem of the book, "You Were About," the poet seems to be remembering, through a series of complex images, a meeting in which she rejected a lover, which would make it a sad meeting. In "Gloss," the poet meets an uncle, which is kind of a tryst, but she meets him through her mother's memory, because he was fatally injured during the war. In "Nevers," the poet considers the horrible cultural tryst between Japan and America in WWII, but also the loving tryst represented by her father's telegram to her mother at the end of the war to say he is coming home. This pun of tryst and triste represents the way Estes develops both sound and sense in an intriguing book of poetry.

The poet Mark Irwin is very concerned with how Estes pursues meaning through sound and visual images in his essay "'Ethereal Streaked by the Real:' Desire, Language, and Memory in Three Poems by Angie Estes." Irwin speaks of Estes's ability to "renew love's violent memory through language." He also very clearly outlines the poet's habit of juxtaposing "real events . . . with metaphysical concepts of memory, time, and desire that she transforms through language." Finally, Irwin suggests that Estes is a visual artist who paints with words.

In her essay "'Words Remain *en Pointe*:' Angie Estes's Choreographic Poetics," B. K. Fischer adds a new dimension to the consideration of Estes's poetry. She argues that "dance is a structural analogy in Estes's work." Indeed, Fischer asserts that dance is more structurally germane to Estes's poetry than literary references. Estes's use of dance is not only a source of imagery, according to Fischer, but also provides "figures for movement of lineation, pacing, extension and juxtaposition."

In "'*Visibile Parlare*': Ekphrastic Images in the Poetry of Angie Estes," I argue that because Estes is not writing narrative poetry, her work challenges the traditional notion that ekphrastic poetry speaks for mute works of art. Instead, Estes employs works of art as images in an effort to cooperate with those masterpieces to move audiences from one emotional state, or state of being, to another. I then examine the way Estes employs art to broaden the cultural and emotional scope of her work in all of her books of poetry.

In "Ready to Sing: Angie Estes's *Enchantée*," Christopher Spaide echoes Stephanie Burt in his claim that Estes's poetry is a kind of expanded version of the Baroque. However, he argues that this is the first book in which Estes envisions Baroque's possible failure. He also claims that *Enchantée* is unusual in Estes's work in the extent to which the poet gives us a glimpse of her life. Finally, Spaide suggests that perhaps both the strength and the weakness of Estes's art is its use of art as a recurring image.

Together these essays explore the way Angie Estes's poetry is both complex and infinitely approachable. Her poetry is complex because of the way she employs sound and what might be referred to as poetic images, such as italics or dance, to weave together verbal pictures through a pattern of association, which explores a sensibility that often moves the reader to an emotional level that transcends logic. Her poetry is approachable because she writes about poetic emotions, such as memory and grief, that are common to the human experience, and she does so by using works of art within her poetry, which are established cultural symbols of emotional profundity. One travels a complex linguistic journey when working through Estes's poetry, but she is careful to guide her readers through the trip with both sound and sense. Her poems are indeed a space where experience happens, experience that both enriches and enlarges the vision of her readers.

Notes

1. Angie Estes. *"Lieu De Moxie-Mémoire."* *Parole* (Oberlin: Oberlin College Press, 2018), 3.
2. Stephanie Burt. "In Every Generation: A Response to Mark Edmundson." *The Boston Review*, July 1, 2013. Online. Available at http://bostonreview.net/blog/every-generation-response-mark-edmundson
3. Estes, *"Lieu De Moxie-Mémoire,"* 3. .
4. Ibid.
5. Ibid.
6. Ibid.
7. John Donne. *The Complete Poetry and Selected Prose*, ed. Charles M. Coffin (New York: Random House, 1952), 252.
8. Angie Estes. *Tryst* (Oberlin: Oberlin College Press, 2009), 34.
9. Ibid.
10. Ibid., 33.
11. Ibid., 33–34.
12. Stephanie Burt. "Nearly Baroque." *The Boston Review*, April 11, 2014. Online. Available at http://bostonreview.net/poetry/stephen-burt-nearly-baroque
13. Samuel Johnson. *The Lives of the English Poets of Great Britain and Ireland and a Criticism of their Works* (Dublin: J. Moore, 1795), 11.
14. Donne, 13–14.
15. Estes, *Tryst*, 34.
16. Valerie Eliot and John Haffenden, eds. *The Letters of T. S. Eliot, Volume 3* (New Haven: Yale University Press, 2012), 233.

DAVID YOUNG

Angie Estes
Five Pleasures

I hope that people still read poetry for the pleasures it can provide. It's true that the world is a vale of shadow and sorrow where poets must wrestle with the demons and dark angels of racism, sexism, militarism, poverty, disease, homophobia, and xenophobia. Most of us wouldn't have them do otherwise, though we may sometimes feel impatient while being lectured about problems of which we're already deeply aware.

It's possible that some readers turn to poems that simply confirm their beliefs and strengthen their self-righteousness. There may be a kind of mild pleasure in that, but I'm in search of something more powerful and startling. "Surprised by joy,"[1] said Wordsworth. Who doesn't hope for that from time to time? It's a lesson I think one can learn from the Chinese poets of the past. Long after the social issues they struggled with have dated and lost immediacy, their ability to transcend suffering and turn sorrow inside out lures us as readers. To wrestle the demon and win: that, apparently, does not lose its attraction and validity.

Unapologetically, then, I want to explore some of the pleasures that Angie Estes offers her readers. Her poems may make demands on us—many of them need rereading and pondering before they yield their full delights—but they offer rewards that make them stand out from the work of many of her contemporaries.

1. Pleasure in Language

This is always a factor in poetry, or should be. As Denise Levertov told me once, the marriage of image and music is the secret of poetry's uniqueness; sometimes that union is achieved through a heightened sensibility in language, a foregrounding, if you like, of words and their delights. With Estes, this can take the form of exu-

berant invention, as in the poem "Brief Encounter," where we chase
after the missing word "romance":

> The story is *the only one*
> > *I can tell and the only one I can*
>
> > *never tell,* she says after she has left
> her lover for the last time, in voiceover
>
> to her husband, *the only one I can tell*
> > *and the only one I can never*
>
> > *tell.* "So help me with this,"
> he says, "you're a poetry addict ---
>
> it's Keats: 'When I behold
> > upon the night's starred face
>
> > huge cloudy symbols of
> a high _____' . . . seven letters,
>
> beginning with *r.*" *reading regalia*
> > *rosette rotunda royalty rapture I didn't think*
>
> > *such violent things could happen*
> *to ordinary people,* she says, *radiant*
>
> *raccoon, raveled rivulet raiment*
> > *release* although weeks ago she and her lover
>
> > sat in a dark theatre and watched the preview
> of a film announced in flickering font
>
> on the screen: *Flames of Passion --- Coming*
> > *Shortly.* The chords of Rachmaninoff draw
>
> > dark lines across their faces, cancel
> conversation like the diagonal trains
>
> that slice the rectangular frames of film
> > in two as they arrive and depart
>
> > from Milford Junction station which, once
> the lovers kiss, becomes a soundproof

room *reprise redwing refusal recount rhubarb*
        reserve, reverse rustles refrain Hurrying

        home in the train she sees her face
facing her face in the window, racing

with darkened trees like the fragrant
        pages of a rampant book.[2]

The film's story of an aborted romance is matched with a cascade (rampage?) of "r" words, a waltz with the dictionary, where love of language encourages a scavenger hunt (ransack?) in which the flames of passion (coming soon) reflect (!) a love of words for their own sake. They form a counterpoint to the images from the film, a leavening for its dark romanticism, dividing our attention expertly.

The double action of the romantic plot and the word-game, played for its own sake, is deftly performed by the poem's behavior on the page, not just the italics but the mirrored stanzas, staggered couplets with matching margins. The whole thing feels effortless, despite its complicated scheme.

2. Pleasure in Languages (Plural)

I need a separate category for the delight and discoveries that involve French, Italian, and other foreign tongues in Estes's poetry. We might be uncomfortable with words and phrases from languages we don't know, if we didn't have an expert and confident guide.

A few examples:

        Uncle Osie showed me how to lean
    the chisel into the lathe, make the chair leg
      curve as strips curled off the long rod
of walnut the way Dante's invented verb
dislagarsi makes the mountain of Purgatory rise up
    out of the lake: it un-lakes itself while God keeps
      turning his lathe with a Florentine form
of the verb *torniare* and makes the world above
        inform the world below . . .

        "Evening:"[3]

They are burning the fields in
                    Assisi, unearthing *tartufi* from beneath the Umbrian oaks
for the umpteenth time. So slow

they don't even shuffle, black
                    and swelling, *tartufi* think
only of roots, just as the Islamic call

to prayer, *adhān*, is at the root
                    of the word *permit*, as in *let someone*
hear these words, for which

they will also need *udun*, the word
                    for *ear* . . .

. . . *Che fai di bello oggi. What are you doing*
                    today, Italians ask when they meet

on the streets of Rome, *What do you make*
                    of the beautiful? . . .

"Che Fai de Bello"[4]

The easy back and forth between English and other poetries and cultures charms and relaxes us. It isn't intimidation, as it often seems to be in Eliot and Pound; it's a joyous sharing of discoveries and insights.

I'm especially fond of the moment when Dante has to invent a word, *dislagarsi*, and Estes has to match him, with "un-lakes itself." I also admire the way we get the greeting *che fai de bello* two times, first colloquially and then literally. Lessons about language and about translation are stored in these examples, again as though nothing could be easier.

3. Pleasure in History

I suspect Estes is a voracious reader on the lookout for curiosities from the past worth saving and treasuring:

buried across the barren plateaus
of Provence, where stone altars
chiseled with *FVLGVR CONDITVM*
mark the point where lightning entered
the ground. Around each site, a wall
remains to keep the divine
fire of Jupiter's signature within
the shafts and passageways
of the earth. . . .[5]

This poem goes on to Plutarch on lightning and then to Nijinsky's diaries. We learn from the notes at the back of the book (*Tryst*) that Estes has consulted, among other texts, *Luminous Debris: Reflecting on Vestige in Provence and Languedoc*, by Gustaf Sobin (1999).

To accomplish such delights, the poet must read, glean, ponder, and know how to shape and place such facts. She must also be at ease with Europe and its deep and complicated past. History and poetry have a sometimes fraught relationship; it's nice to see them at ease, personal and impersonal at once, dancing cheek to cheek.

4. Pleasure in Juxtaposition

Metaphor is juxtaposition, of course, delighting simultaneously in likeness and difference. A distinguishing feature of Estes's work is her skillful use of it on both the micro and the macro levels. In the just-cited poem about lightning, for example, it contributes to the texture, "Jupiter's signature,"[6] as well as to the overall structure: the poem moves on from Plutarch on victims of lightning, "whoever is touched / by lightning is invested with divine / powers,"[7] to Nijinsky and his famous madness, diaries, and spectacular leaps. He thought he had "invented a fountain pen / called God."[8] His kindredness with thunderbolt victims is deftly explored and the poem closes by describing a 1939 photograph of him "against a white wall, a foot / and a half above the floor, arms / outstretched and blurred like a hummingbird / hovering at a flower or a man before / a firing squad at close range."[9] The hummingbird and firing squad similes balance the poem's emotional extremes of beauty and suffering, while what seemed an incidental figure, God's signature, comes back to haunt us in the mad dancer's diary. Such architectonics are typical of this poet. As for the hummingbird?"each sip a *jeté* / of light."[10]

Here's another example of the various levels of juxtaposition this poet delights in:

"PER YOUR REQUEST,"

gilded bronze rosettes once pressed
through the Pantheon's dome like stars

filling the coffers of the sky,
and history posed especially

for you, its spree become
repose. From the Janiculum hill

across the Tiber, you watched
the aureole settle around

its nipple as if a flying saucer
nestled among the rising

stones and called it
home . . .[11]

The juxtaposings involve words—"posed" and "repose"—and metaphors—nipple, flying saucer—as the entire poem opens out into a skyscape of Rome:

Wisteria still hopes

over every wall, holding it
in place, while the lantern of Sant'Ivo

screws into the sky. When the snakes
sacred to Asclepius arrived

on Isola Tiberina, they made themselves
at home on the floors of the temple

dedicated to healing: dogs were trained
to lick and snakes to flicker

their tongues over any ailing
part of the body. You always loved

the way a crow's
caw caw caw hangs

in the sky like a claw,
a crowbar that pries open

the day: a posse of roses coming
to possess you.[12]

Everywhere I look there are pairings—posse/possess, crow/crow-
bar, caw/claw, lick/flicker, rosettes/roses—that reinforce and com-
plicate this dazzling scene, a Roman dawn. It's as though such jux-
taposings were the most natural thing in the world. But they require
exceptional care and thought, especially if they are to achieve the
brilliant consistency of texture that Angie Estes is known for.

5. Pleasure in Music

When a poet has a good ear—such as Stevens, Wilbur, Bishop, He-
aney, Charles Wright—we know it right away because the verbal
music often strikes us first, even ahead of our making sense of what
we're reading and hearing. Sometimes the music is so foregrounded,
as in Hopkins, as to threaten to drown out the imagery and thought.
More typically it coexists with those attributes. Here's our poet in
an especially musical frame of mind:

"NIGH CLIME"

Who remembers the waving hinge, how
the spine of a book or elm could limn
the locale of *gee* and *hmm* and *oh*, tingle
with the *nom* of its genome chill as if Patsy Cline
were at the helm of the angelic galleon, singing
I'm crazy, crazy for feeling so blue . . .[13]

I'm not sure what it *means*. I just know that it's partly about music
and is music itself:

When the long

is gone and the curtain opens
its glee like leaves in April, we'll mingle
like scenery and ogle o'er ego and e'en, the glim
of ago.

We still come helloing up the lingo
hill, its chenille lawn aching
with echo: omen, a lien
on our line. Lean your nog
against mine own and lift the hem
of home, not inchmeal but once: your chin
on its agile cello, your leg nigh
in the niche of time.[14]

It's a love poem, it's full of puns and play. Saying it out loud is the best way to see what it's up to. This kind of playfulness with word-music may be found everywhere in Estes's poetry. Sometimes it almost gets out of hand: see the poem "Pallino, Pallone," also in *Enchantée*, and originally, I'm happy to admit, in *FIELD*.

My list of pleasures could be extended, but I think I will rest my case. Few poets offer us such consistent riches and delights. Maybe we should call her Angie Ecstasy. Her discoveries and insights, so nimbly shaped and communicated, raise a standard in this gloomy world to which I am proud to pledge allegiance.

Works Cited

Bloom, Harold, and Lionel Trilling, eds. *Romantic Poetry and Prose*. Oxford: Oxford University Press, 1973.
Estes, Angie. *Enchantée*. Oberlin: Oberlin College Press, 2013.
Estes, Angie. *Tryst*. Oberlin: Oberlin College Press, 2009.

Notes

1. Harold Bloom and Lionel Trilling, eds. *Romantic Poetry and Prose* (Oxford: Oxford University Press, 1973), 229.
2. Angie Estes. *Enchantée* (Oberlin: Oberlin College Press, 2013), 18–19.
3. Ibid., 34.
4. Ibid., 51–52.

5. Angie Estes. *Tryst* (Oberlin: Oberlin College Press, 2009), 23.

6. Ibid., 23.

7. Ibid., 23.

8. Ibid., 23.

9. Ibid., 24.

10. Ibid., 24.

11. Estes, *Enchantée*, 3.

12. Ibid., 3–4.

13. Ibid., 15.

14. Ibid., 15.

JULIANNE BUCHSBAUM

Beyond Lyric
Review of Voice-Over

The poems in Angie Estes's *Voice-Over* reveal a place in language where past and present, meaning and music converge in unusual ways. The book, as a whole, engages in a dialectic between paradigms of classical culture and displacements of personal identity, as if the speakers of individual poems were searching for a temporary stay against chaos or the "phantom pain" of a part of the self that's missing though "its home / in the brain is not" ("Lilac Fugue").[1] Estes employs a rhetoric of ruins and runes (puns, homophones, assonance, internal rhymes, and etymology are some of her favorite devices to parse the path from Point A to Point Elsewhere in a poem) in order to anatomize and reconstruct a landscape of eros-haunted culture. Like a subtle post-fin-de-siècle pentimento, Estes's words half-reveal, half-conceal the raw material beneath ornate overlays of culture, which only makes those overlays more sublime. The poems seem driven by a quest to understand and locate the self through art, music, architecture, and language, to find a brief respite amid the ruptures and spoilage of a culture where the self can "ris[e] from the / ruins of what we've become" (*"Roma Caput Mundi"*).[2]

Memory, the past, and history become sets of architectural spaces, rooms in which the windows open out onto something infinitely larger and richer than the given conditions of our mundane lives, something "impossible / to reach from here," yet longed for with passion.[3] In "Entrance to an Imaginary Villa," for example, the speaker contemplates a littoral zone where the terrene touches upon and suggests the transcendent—here, the "verdigris air" of Pompeii is not only the air of an ancient occluded past but also merely an illusion of air, therefore, impossible to breathe or touch. The poem then switches over to a series of questions beautifully phrased and haunting: "let" becomes "letter" becomes "slits" in "Is there a room / to let, a letter / waiting, a bird who slits / the air?"[4] The tone of sadness suggests that the deracinated speaker was trying to recover a lost sense of self through knowledge of the past or communion with ghosts of ancient Italy. Indeed, the words "room" and "home" are repeated throughout the poem until the speaker, in the end, seems to find release from this longing through the open windows of vows and vowels.

While many of the poems seem concerned with getting from a "here" to an otherworldly, remote, and perhaps sublime "there," always it is language that leads Estes from one place to another, and a common strategy of the poems is for Estes to start off with a word or phrase, meditate on its sounds and etymology, and trace a net of related images. For example, in "Classical Order," after quoting from Corinthians and then describing Corinthian columns by comparing them to skeletal vertebrae, the speaker then meditates on the etymology of vertebrae ("vertere"), then on the biblical tale of St. Veronica and the origins of her name, and in the end she brings it all home by evoking "all the motel rooms across America / that do not want / to be disturbed."[5]

Language appears in many of the poems as a screen between human understanding and the unmediated world of things, yet it also expresses a profound longing to heal that diremption, a longing that is epistemological in origin but takes on an ardency that can become quite frank in its eroticism, as when the speaker of "Rhapsody" says "No one says it / anymore, my darling"—the discourse of romanticism interpolated into a consciousness of its obsolescence.[6] Estes has a sensibility that hears and sees language everywhere in the world, as later in the poem an owl's call becomes "Who cooks for you . . . Who looks / for you?"[7] (or, for example, "the deer / thrown back like the s / in *swan*,"[8] or "the squirrel . . . who curves his tail forward // to cover his body and become / the initial that stands // for his name" ["Vermeer Fever"]).[9] The beauty of such observations is juxtaposed against an awareness of death, culture, and history that opens the poems out into something more meaningful than a merely personal lyric.

Voice-Over is a collection of poems worth reading just for the vivid materiality and musical effects of the language alone (i.e., lines like "pleated ruffle, tutu // touching base / with a dewclaw" and internal rhymes like "Chartreuse," "ruse" and "hens," "Firenze"). However, Estes is too restless a thinker to be satisfied with "the conclusion / of the cardinal: pretty, pretty, pretty, / pretty—" and asks, "but pretty what?" ("Rhapsody").[10] Estes is not content to mesmerize but uses language to conduct an all-out strip search of culture in which the poet becomes a kind of physician or metaphysician of language, redeeming and cleansing it of its exhaustions and consolidating its various *membra disjecta.*

One of the things I enjoy most about Estes's work is her success at negotiating a balance between intellect and feeling, meaning and music, philology and faith. She mixes many different levels of diction, plus words from different languages (French, Latin, Gaelic) and often balances a precise, detached, almost cold clarity of imagery, such as "Le Corbusier's statue of Mary / in the chapel at Ronchamp" against something with more emotional urgency as in "Dear Maria, / I have to talk to you." Another example is "Say Merveille," a paean to Josephine Baker in which sweet, ripe images of honeysuckle blossoms and bananas are played against sharper-edged images such as dark stars, bees, and discord. The language play, where Estes switches fluidly between French and English, playing with puns such as "say" and "c'est" and "la mer, ma / mere, nightmare" and "Dis aster, dark / star" creates a lush, compelling, multi-languaged surface texture that seems to reflect a sort of polymorphous pleasure in the different possibilities of languages and languaged identities.[11] In a world in which "[m]usic / is what is left of luster, heading / west," we need more of such writing.

Notes

1. Angie Estes. *Voice-Over* (Oberlin: Oberlin College Press, 2002), 13.
2. Ibid., 41.
3. Ibid., 7.
4. Ibid., 7.
5. Ibid., 18.
6. Ibid., 17.
7. Ibid., 17.
8. Ibid., 10.
9. Ibid., 24.
10. Ibid., 18.
11. Ibid., 22.

LEAH FALK

Memory, Grief, and the Linguistic Artifact in Angie Estes's Poems

Angie Estes used to give her students an exercise: go home and turn on a recording of a song in a language you don't understand. Listen to it a few times, then transcribe the sounds you hear in the foreign words. Make of the sounds—nonsensical to you—the closest possible English words. Finally, with the materials you've gathered, make a poem. The results force the writer to look closely at the seemingly irreducible compound of language: its component parts, rhythm and sound. *Comprehend me*, it begs, and we oblige. Embedded in this almost surrealist prompt is what could be considered the thesis of Estes's work: when in doubt, consult the word, its sound, etymology, history. Coming to Estes's poems, we find the shared phonology of *Rome* and *roam*, the anagrammatic possibilities of *starlings*, the English poem hiding inside a listening of *The Marriage of Figaro* by a non-native Italian speaker. These are the marks of a poet who assumes that there is truth in the very letters with which we build words, who makes poems with the hypothesis that language is a better archivist of human history and memory than are actual humans—falsifiers, erasers, and equivocators that we are.

All poets lean on the music of language, but Estes employs a habit I'll call corporeality. She relies on the idea that the bodies of words are not coincidental but rather the results of our human processes of collecting, recording, and forgetting. They are tiny arguments about the procedures of history. At the junctions where the poem would reveal its emotional core, where a lesser poet would be tempted to explain, she often turns to the word as artifact, using its story as a mirror for the poem's own. In her six books, Estes's poems have evolved to use this habit as a kind of air traffic control, a series of guides through difficult ideas or emotions. In her early work, poems often follow sound toward meaning, sometimes letting the latter emerge surrealistically and by accident, as in her own student exercise. In her second book, *Voice-Over*, she opens with "Hors

D'Oeuvre," which begins by letting *Alyssum* side-eye *asylum* and *jus* blur into *juste*. This is wordplay, but it is serious:

> . . . each *madame* sings
> *avoir* in the key of middle
> need, which sounds so much
> like *au revoir,* you step back in
> for *champagne* and adores,
> to hear what's missed
> pronounced again in conjugated
> light, as if to see again
> is to have.[1]

Estes arrives here by cultivating the naiveté of the non-native speaker. There's wicked delight, she suggests, in mistakes, as in the title of the poem above, punny if pronounced like a non-French speaker. Estes senses that something existentially important, something true, lives in that mistake-space. Rather than be grounds for error, the similarity in sound between *avoir* and *au revoir* is taken as a case for their relationship, permission to cross the gulf of mystery between their meanings. Exploring that space means preserving, simultaneously, the experiences of understanding and not-understanding. As she puts it, to both see again and to have.

In many poems, the gulf between words like *hem* and *home, nigh* and *niche,* the sense of sonic return that makes a rhyme pleasing, in the uncanny valleys of language, Estes finds that a single word can transpose reality or provide a clue to another consciousness. In *Enchantée*'s "Note," the speaker is informed that someone has "found my mother *wondering / in the garage.*"[2] The error animates the poem, as Estes traces a line of inquiry the speaker's mother can, presumably, no longer pursue, about what happens to our desires after we lose the memory that makes them ours:

> In paradise,
> Dante says, we will have only a memory
> of having had a memory, now lost
> like the photograph of my mother's great
> grandfather printed from a negative made
> from a photograph of a negative, which we
> Xeroxed for keeps: it's the same old
> story of the Perseids, their gray hair
> streaking the sky the way ethereal
> is streaked by real[3]

The misheard word opens up a parallel universe, one buried just beneath the surface of our speech. There, we can enter the habitat of our unarticulated fears: here, that fear is our desperation to remember and fear of the day we'll forget ["my friend's father / kept asking, What if my mother dies / again? What, I thought, if she slips off / like a glove"[4]]. Estes understands that our language's built-in redundancies betray a lining of superstition in our thoughts: when we say something twice, make extra copies, understand meaning despite a missing letter, we're being shown both what we consider precious and what we most fear.

Worlds and systems of belief (". . . the way ethereal / is streaked by real"[5]) can also collide in these apparent linguistic accidents. The fun Estes has with the permeable borders of language has a mortal edge. In "Entrance to an Imaginary Villa," she writes: "How easily the edge / of this world becomes / the edge of the next. . . ."[6] In the poem, that edge is at once a visual border, in the painting of a house on the bedroom wall, creating a space that can be imagined but not accessed. It's also a linguistic one: the unyielding painting contains an essence "[f]lat / as literal translation";[7] and it's a mortal one—the world to come converging on the world of the living, the real "streaking" the ethereal. Imagining Estes imagining edges, you can see why she so liberally quotes St. Augustine and Dante throughout *Voice-Over*. "Open and close me . . . like a vowel,"[8] she tells us Augustine prayed. It's human life as vowel space, the soft sound of flexible length and mutable shape kept between two hard, finite barriers—the uncertain space between certainties—that Estes promises to explore by taking her lens to the spaces between what we say and what we mean to say.

If our brains are so intent on leaping, the borders of our lives become so porous, and our meaning so difficult to make precise, Estes reckons that the history of our efforts at speech—at all expression—contains an enormous margin of error and by extension a lot of ghosts, many unrealized worlds. Maybe a lot of what, in "Entrance," "roams / around its rising rooms, repeating / O's and making vows to slide / the window close/ to closed."[9] Those failed attempts at connection mean we are always trying again to communicate, to feel full. Many of the poems in *Voice-Over* concern themselves with the movements we make to populate emptiness: the emptiness of waiting, or uncertainty, or the voids in memory or history or imagination. In "*Musique d'Ameublement*" she begins with Erik Satie's idea of "furniture music":

He said it would fill up
The silence that sometimes
Descends on guests as they sip
Sherry on the sofa, just before dinner
Begins, that the sound of furniture
Being moved would be enough
To furnish those rooms
We wait in, just as the sound
Of lovers making furniture
Move in the adjoining suite
Is sometimes enough
To fill our room too.[10]

The idea of "filler" or mere "content" is ugly—no artist, one supposes, sets out to make "furniture music." But here, what at first merely fills can suddenly furnish: what was meant to stave off awkwardness or boredom can accidentally inspire or even arouse. The poem's long strophe, which "fills" the page, also makes subtle a shift from one sense of "fill" to another: what begins as a packing, an apparent obscuring of emptiness, becomes something building toward sexual and existential satisfaction ("Is sometimes enough / To fill our room too"). Only by the risky act of putting expression out into space do we make such "filling" a possibility.

The artist's impulse to make use of empty space may be, like Satie's, ironically static, or it may be dynamic and existential, as Estes explores in "Lilac Fugue." She recounts Rilke's belief that "repeated notes rising / from the organ for centuries / inside Notre Dame / had rounded the curves / of every arch—that there are strains / of music, musical sprains. . . ."[11] From humans' other uses of emptiness—monks' drawings in the margins of illuminated manuscripts, the phantom feeling in a lost limb—Estes ventures that one of the problems with being human is that we lose a lot with every step, far more than we manage to maintain. Language—and art—keeps track for us. Rather than claim that it puts our mark on the world, Estes might say that art archives our efforts, the clamor of our desperation to say something about the world we live in. Hence the end of "Lilac Fugue":

And what
does the beech tree inscribe
on the sky with its flourish of copper
serifs? Each angle

of the conductor's baton
still holding its place
in air, the late evening sky
still lighted by its white
crossed scars of flight.[12]

Here, Estes modifies an old poet's wish: for language to enact and shape as well as it adorns, for our artistic gestures, despite their fragility, to have lingered somehow in nature. Such wishes become more urgent when language has something personal to do.

In *Enchantée*, her fifth collection, the mortal edge becomes the whole landscape. The need for language to act and give shape, to carry—to be, almost, a spell—becomes vital. As translator Peter Cole notes about Kabbalistic writing, "Poems not only depict a mystical process, they produce it."[13] The narrative touchstone of a father's death gives Estes's careful revisions—that *see again*—of meaning something to grapple with, to grasp. They've encountered a sort of destiny: *comprehend me*, grief says to them, *translate me*. Grief is a song in a language nobody understands, like the accident that makes *au revoir* converge with *avoir*, it has a vague notation, happening somewhere unexpected in the brain. Here the amorphousness of grief throws into relief the searching articulations—etymological, phonological, anagrammatic—that by now have become her hallmark.

Enchantée begins by calling our attention, again, to the omissions of history and memory. An epigraph from a map legend outlines "Structures that are visible, Structures not visible but about whose position we are certain, and Structures thought to have existed."[14] This legend, found on an excavation map below Rome's Church of Saint Cecilia, is also the legend to the book: Estes signals that she will be notating emotional objects that are partially obscured, hypothesized, or imagined.

"Per Your Request," the book's first poem, brings all three of these elements together. Addressed to someone lost, it begins by evoking a favored moment in Rome, one that the addressee might have specifically chosen if asked. The title of the poem is also the dependent clause from which the imagery of the moment gains its momentum:

gilded bronze rosettes once pressed
through the Pantheon's dome like stars

filling the coffers of the sky,
and history posed especially

for you, its spree become
repose.[15]

As the poem moves out of memory and into the present moment,
Estes drops the lullaby-like rhythm and steady rhyme. But "Wisteria
still hopes / over every wall, holding it / in place. . . ."[16] The phys-
ical, here botanical, serves as an armature for memory, for those
visible structures whose position is hazy. As she'll do with sound,
she sets up the image as a guidepost for making sense of what's hap-
pened. As she does repeatedly in the book, Estes then veers into
history and myth:

When the snakes
sacred to Asclepius arrived

on Isola Tiberina, they made themselves
at home on the floors of the temple

dedicated to healing: dogs were trained
to lick and snakes to flicker

their tongues over any ailing
part of the body.[17]

If the "hoping" wisteria provides some support for the shakiness of
memory, especially in a place revisited, then ancient history grounds
the speaker even further, keeps her at clinical distance. The long his-
tory of Rome compensates for the fact that personal history is eas-
ily rewritten. Against such uncertainty, better to have as a touch-
stone a place where history seems nonnegotiable, even if by its
nature, it's riddled with omissions.

Toward the poem's end, the seams found in the material of the
present and ancient past not only do the work of holding together
memory of the poem's addressee but also convey them into the

future, a future which almost certainly includes death or absence: "You always loved // the way a crow's / *caw caw caw* hangs // in the sky like a claw, / a crowbar that pries open // the day: a posse of roses coming / to possess you."[18] The roses, along with the visual of the final "s" in "possess" closing "posse" open the poem to the possibility of a new memory in an old place, while providing the "you" with a pathway out.

Here, Estes sets the stage for the collection: language, rather than directly signifying, will cluster around meaning and memory in locations of grief as in a scatterplot. At the same time, she pursues her own weakness for that earlier poet's wish seen in *Voice-Over*: the desire to populate the spaces memory, history, imagination, and plain human failing seem to have left empty. The activation point for these new poems is often the crossroads between the two, the paradox of attempting to refine one's meaning when faced with an apparent dearth of it. A flock of starlings in "I Want to Talk About You" shifts meanings as it shifts shape in the late afternoon sky: in the space of a few lines, the birds are "like a blanket tossed into the sky," "a cowl that lengthens to a woolen scarf wrapping // and wrapping . . . thousands of single black notes . . . the bodies of suicides . . . words falling // out of a sentence."[19] They evoke "extended cadenzas to pieces / that never get played," then fall "unable to rise the way a wave / nearing shore will crest, something on the tip of its tongue // thrown back before it breaks and splays." This near-graphomanic backdrop, where the spectacle of a changing physical shape wreaks havoc with the poet's figure-making brain, is actually, as the title suggests, the ideal space to speak of the missing "you."

The father, the object of grief, doesn't appear directly in relation to the speaker until the collection's fifth poem, "Bon Voyage," and then seemingly in a thought experiment generated by the Proust epigraph Estes includes: "*People do not die for us immediately, but remain bathed in a sort of aura of life [. . .] through which they continue to occupy our thoughts in the same way as when they were alive. It is as though they were traveling abroad.*"[20] Estes begins by imagining the new daily habits of her father who "never traveled / to France, but now lives / in Paris on the rue Mouffetard."[21] But although Estes fills the space of her father's absence with faithfully imagined details—rare steak and a bottle of Vacqueyras, followed by a wedge of Rocquefort—of his existence "abroad" in what is becoming memory, that thought experiment cannot help but reconnect with real memory, the distant experienced past. Of course, the bridge between the two for Estes, the wisteria hoping of this poem, is another linguistic artifact: in particular, a nursery rhyme.

> Later, as he walks
> across the city, he snaps his fingers, singing
> *Hey diddle diddle, The cat and the fiddle,*
> *The cow jumped over the moon,* the way
> he came up the stairs to wake me
> when I was a child, keeping
> in mind what Augustine said
> of memory: *With my tongue silent*
> *and my throat making no sound, I can sing*
> *what I wish.*[22]

Hey Diddle Diddle is both bridge and hinge: bridge because it permits the speaker to travel back with her father to the past instead of existing in her conjuring of his life after death. It is a hinge because it turns the poem toward hope and questioning: the speaker tries to summon her father as easily as he once summoned the nursery rhyme, tries to "sing / what I wish" of him. But even as it seems poised to reassure us that memory is part of the brain's music-making, its art, the placement of Augustine's dictum draws tension between Estes's careful childhood flashback and the father's imagined afterlife. What's real, our past memories of the dead or the new imaginings to which we summon them after they're gone? To what extent does our evoking the dead in their absence, often for our comfort, alter them irrevocably? Estes's vision alters her father, who in the poem "reads *Le Monde* / without knowing any French."[23] But even after touching on a place of childhood comfort, broadcast by the words of the rhyme, she still returns him to his adventure abroad. Refreshing language and narrative, even if they displace or alter the dead, are the only tools to drive forward from that stalled spot, the vague white space of grief: "In spring, he plans / to go to London, thinks that perhaps / if the weather is good, my mother / might come."[24]

It's with this kind of calculation about the interaction between sound and memory, presence and absence, that Estes fulfills the hunger of her own early poems and then some: she grants her own wish to be Rilke's imagined musical detritus, lingering materially after a departure. But also, crucially, her poems inhabit future space, relying on the generative nature of sound to fill painful absences and build new worlds. In *Enchantée*'s penultimate poem, "Almost Autumn," she writes:

> . . . we found out
> what it was like to spend an entire season
> in the Perseids, how God must have felt
> creating the stars in an initial O, illuminated
>
> in a fifteenth century manuscript in Siena. So many
> stars to touch on the iPad of the night, to name
> as each turned into light: *wear, were,*
>
> *never, ere.*[25]

Listen, Estes says, how with the power of the sound we create the world, and then look at how we've managed to capture it, improbably, in writing and naming. To make sound is necessarily to be active, to enact and enliven. She reminds us of this in *Enchantée*'s last poem, "Recall," beginning with a woman squeezing a trout and instructing it to pronounce the vowels *a e i o u*. One's reminded of Rudyard Kipling's "How the Alphabet Was Made," one of many origin fables of writing, in which Taffy explains to her father that a picture of a carp's mouth symbolizes the sound *ah*. This is the beginning of writing, being able to give a body to language. ". . . it is impossible // to think the vowel sound *ah* without / tensing, tightening the vocal chords: *we read* ah / *and the voice is ready to sing.*"[26] Packed in that singing, Estes has shown us, are memory, grief, and desire. It's the poet's privilege to take the fleeting world such singing makes and give it a body, write it down, hope it lasts.

Notes

1. Angie Estes. *Voice-Over* (Oberlin: Oberlin College Press, 2002), 3.
2. Angie Estes. *Enchantée* (Oberlin: Oberlin College Press, 2013), 26.
3. Estes, *Enchantée*, 26–27.
4. Ibid., 26.
5. Ibid., 27.
6. Estes, *Voice-Over*, 7.
7. Ibid., 8.
8. Ibid., 7.
9. Ibid., 8.
10. Estes, *Voice-Over*, 21.

11. Ibid., 13.
12. Ibid., 14.
13. Peter Cole. *The Poetry of Kabbalah* (New Haven: Yale University Press, 2012), ix.
14. Estes, *Enchantée*, v.
15. Ibid., 3.
16. Ibid. 3
17. Ibid., 3–4.
18. Ibid., 4.
19. Ibid., 5.
20. Ibid., 11.
21. Ibid., 11.
22. Ibid., 11–12.
23. Ibid., 11.
24. Ibid., 12.
25. Ibid., 62.
26. Ibid., 64.

AHREN WARNER

A Lawless Proposition
Angie Estes and the Line

> . . . the dove
>   more banner than bird, which from
> the beginning was the word for
>   *verb* – part sky, part earth, part
> of speech expressing action, occurrence,
>   existence.

— Angie Estes, Proverbs[1]

I want to begin with an observation. Like most poets, I spend a significant amount of time teaching the craft of writing poetry. I also seem to spend a disproportionate amount of that time standing at a photocopier with one of Angie Estes's books. In fact, pretty much any time I am teaching a seminar or workshop on the "poetic line," I find myself turning to Estes's work as an example of the strange, philosophically troubling and yet commonplace practice that is the lyric line and the line-break.

In what follows, I want to examine three of Estes's poems— "Takeoff" from *Tryst* (2009) and "Paramour" and "On Yellowed Velvet" from *Chez Nous* (2005)—paying attention to the very particular line-breaks of these poems and the stakes—emotional, epistemological, technical—they put in play. I will suggest that Estes tends to deploy the line-break as a quiet disruption of the unity of both the subject of representation and the lyric "I," that such line-breaks unsettle and solicit both the possibility of the poem as referential and radically destabilize it as an event of interlocution. It is because of Estes's talent for deploying the line-break to the fullest of its innately radical potential that I go back to Estes again and again as an exemplary practitioner of the line itself.

Before turning to the poems, a passing word on my title might be necessary. "A lawless proposition" is a label that the French philosopher Alain Badiou uses to describe the poem in his *Handbook of Inaesthetics*.[2] There Badiou operates a wonderful transformation of the old Platonic rejection of poetry as either mere mimesis or, worse, degenerate deception into an argument for the very worth of poetry. "What poetry forbids is discursive thought,"[3] he writes, arguing that, in opposition to either the matheme or philosophical discourse, and "presuming the existence of a thinking of the poem, or that the poem is itself a form of thought, this thought is inseparable from the sensible. It is a thought *that cannot be discerned or separated as a thought.* We could say that the poem is an unthinkable thought."[4] Badiou goes on:

> Plato banished the poem because he suspected that poetic thought cannot be the thought of thought . . . we will welcome the poem because it permits us to forgo the claim that the singularity of a thought can be replaced by the thinking of this thought.[5]

What I will come to suggest is that Estes's deployment of the line often constitutes the manifestation of the poem as a kind of thinking that cannot be thought as anything other than the poetic event it constitutes. It seems to me that it is in this sense that Estes's work witnesses the unsettling singularity of the poetic line itself.

> . . . and so Delilah sings *Mon coeur*
> *s'ouvre à ta voix, My heart opens*
> *at your voice,* but then must cut
> Samson's hair because he prefers
> God to her, Miss Taken
> for Granted.
>
> — "Takeoff"[6]

"Miss Taken / for Granted," "Mistaken for Granted," "Miss *taken*"— the question here is *which* of these do *you* hear, understand, or feel?

One critical model of the line-break, elucidated by John Hollander and later glossed by Jonathan Culler, is of the line-break as a kind of sequential amplification of meaning. In his case, Hollander is writing of the following lines from Milton:

> Satan, now first inflamed with rage, came down,
> The Tempter ere th'Accuser of mankind,
> To wreck on innocent frail man his loss
> Of that first Battle, and his flight to Hell. . . .[7]

As Culler glosses Hollander, the line-break after "loss" produces a reading of such "loss" as "man's fall,"[8] before, as Hollander writes, the next line "reveals the true antecedent, but the ambiguity of the pronoun reflects the fact that, in the poem, Satan's loss is not only the type of Adam's, but a cause of it";[9] the line-break thus momentarily divides the syntactic sense of a phrase before uniting it into a single, amplified meaning.

Yet I am not sure that such a model does justice to either the craft at work in these lines of Estes (or, indeed, Milton's) or the intensity of their affect as a poetic event. Writing on Mallarmé, Jacques Derrida points us to another potential model, one in which the radical undecidability that poetic space (here, the line-break) might produce

> is not caused . . . by some enigmatic equivocality, some inexhaustible ambivalence of a word in a "natural" language. . . . What counts here is not the lexical richness, the semantic infiniteness of a word or concept, its depth or breadth, the sedimentation that has produced inside it two contradictory layers of signification (continuity and discontinuity, inside and outside, identity and difference, etc.). What counts here is the formal or syntactical *praxis* that composes and decomposes it.[10]

The syntactical practice that seems at play in the lines from Estes's "Takeoff" cited above might be located precisely in the line-break between "Miss Taken" and "for Granted." This line-break provides an extra quotient of insulation to "Miss Taken"; it provides the elongation of a natural pause that forces us to more fully hear the intricate poetic structure on offer. The internal cadence of preceding lines—"*coeur*" / "hair" / "prefers" / "her"—colludes with the comma before "Miss Taken" to mark the latter phrase out, to isolate it as an independent clause that stands and *means* before we have progressed to "for Granted." The intrinsic relations between piety, male aggression, male *possession*, female desire, and identity (has Miss been "taken" or is she "taken" with someone?) that are conjured into play are produced as affective events in the perfectly poised music of a few well-chosen words. And then, of course, the reader falls from the biblical, from high culture to the contemporary vernacular, to both "taken for granted" and "Miss Taken for Granted."

Yet such a sketch of these lines risks masking the more radical nature of the line-break. As the line-break "composes and decomposes" these multiple meanings and affects, it does so as synchronous and simultaneous rather than sequential phenomena. The undecidability of Miss Taken as a violated or infatuated identity, of being "mistaken" or "taken for granted" is not a question to be deciphered, not an "or" but a profoundly radical "and" that conjures the Heraclitean heresy that something might both "be" and "not be" simultaneously and, in being (and not being) so, contravenes the central tenets of Aristotelian logic.

In "Takeoff," as well as in many other poems, Estes emphatically deploys the line-break as generative of synchronous semantic and affective pluralities, as subversive conjunctions that both compose and decompose.

> . . . of San Gimignano fallen
> on its side, lines grazing out
> and back like the lines of
> this poem, like cows coming
> home, where Italo Svevo swore
> to his new wife, Livia: *I will love you*
> *forever, as far as the fin de siècle*
> *will allow.* He meant to be
> diagonal like agony, to outlast
> the flat leaves of the hollyhock, which hasten
> to lace.[11]

From this perspective, these lines from Estes's "Takeoff" might act as both a declaration and demonstration of how she deploys what Mallarmé called the "printless distance" of the page as, simultaneously, an intervention, interruption, *and* constitution of the poetic line. Moreover, it seems to me that Estes's deployment of the line-break in this passage is also a lyric embodiment of the same kind of disruptive tension between separation and union that the poem is simultaneously thinking in a romantic register. In this sense, Estes's image of "lines grazing out and back" might also implicate the "lines of this poem" as intimately connected to the particular act of saying "I will love you" that the reader also witnesses in the poem.

The essential point is that the poem does not simply present "lines grazing out and back like the lines of this poem" but instead *offers us* "lines grazing out / and back." San Gimignano has "fallen / on its side," its lines are "grazing out and back," and the semantic meaning of this phrase—without the intervention of the line-break—is of lines that graze in one direction and then, without interruption, arc back to return to a perspectival point of genesis. Yet the continuity of this movement of lines *is not* uninterrupted; rather the line-break breaks the movement of these lines so that they are "grazing out / and back." In a very real sense, the reader feels such lines moving outward; the movement of these lines is centrifugal, a movement *away*. It is only as the reader moves across the line-break that the reader comes to feel this movement away as the first stage of a moving *toward*; it is only after the intervention of the line-break that the reader understands that to move away is *also* a moving toward, with the emphasis placed on the conjunction "and" in the second line.

Yet such a simplified diagram of the movement of these lines misses the very *affect* of the line-break in question. Returning to the passage from Derrida's *Dissemination* mentioned above, what the reader feels is not a certain "lexical richness" nor the accrual of "two contradictory layers of signification (continuity and discontinuity, inside and outside . . .)" but a certain practice of composition and decomposition: the process of one movement (outward) decomposing into the composition of the opposite movement (inward) that will, and could, never undo the event of a certain outward movement that is still felt as such even as one passes into its opposite.

In this sense, Estes's line-break institutes a feeling of vertigo, a shock of moving and continuing to move in opposite directions simultaneously, and one that brings to mind a rather different passage of Theodor W. Adorno's work than the one Estes cites as an epigraph to *Chez Nous*:

> . . . cognition that is to bear fruit will throw itself to the objects *à fond perdu*. The vertigo which this causes is an *index veri*; the shock of inconclusiveness, the negative as which it cannot help appearing in the frame-covered, never-changing realm, is true for untruth only.[12]

This "grazing out / and back" induces a kind of vertigo in the reader that cannot be reduced to the "shock of inclusiveness," the disorientation of the reader whose mind travels "out" and, over the line-break, only to come back again. What occurs is not the recognition that what comes after the intervention of the line-break completes what comes before, placing misrecognition in a past that yet maintains a certain evocation. Rather what occurs are lines that graze "out / *and* back" simultaneously, perpetually, and the vertigo that the line-break induces in the reader is not one of recognition but of feeling; the shock, not of inconclusiveness, but of a rather Heraclitean dichotomy in which the line both runs outward and does not. It is in this sense that the line-break guarantees that those lines of San Gimignano perpetually run on, and perpetually return, that they constitute a formal and affective performance homologous to the construction of "love" as it is also felt within "Takeoff."

It is, after all, Estes's poem itself that states the homology between the lines of San Gimignano and the problem of *love* as it occurs in "Takeoff." It is the poem itself that tells us that the lines of San Gimignano are like "the lines of / this poem," lines in which "Italo Svevo swore / to his new wife, Livia: *I will love you / forever, as far as the fin de siècle / will allow.*" This declaration and formulation of love also mirrors the formal *affect* of that line-break ("grazing out / and back") that has been under discussion.

Here, again, in these lines readers may feel a certain vertigo as they register the event of these four lines passing into each other. "Italo Svevo swore" and Svevo's vow is defined as maintaining a certain perpetual integrity as the page, that "printless distance," intervenes to define it as discreet, as a solid and solemn promise. Svevo swore "to his new wife, Livia: *I will love you*" and that feeling of a promise as infinite, as defined as unmitigated and unqualified, as the simplicity of a declaration walled off from qualification by the insulation of the line-break is evident. Even as the reader passes into the next line, such a sense of romantic intensity and integrity is maintained—"*I will love you / forever*"—though, it turns out, forever is "*as far as the fin de siècle.*" Here the infinite and absolute gesture of that simple "I will love you" is now absolutely finite: "I will love you until the end of the century," which—given Svevo's historical specificity—may not be very long. And then, of course, such qualification, such a diminishment of that absolute declaration—"I will love you"—becomes "*as far as the fin de siècle / will allow.*"

In these lines, then, the declaration of love "grazes out and back," the *absolute* romantic commitment is also that which is qualified by a historicized periodicity and contingent on what the events of that period might allow. Italo Svevo's "I will love" is simultaneously felt as absolute, continuing *ad infinitum* into the infinitely blank continuance of the page, and absolutely conditional, limited both by the "*fin de siècle*" and that which it allows. This love, which is also "diagonal agony"—much like San Gimignano has "fallen / on its side"—is both unending and always-already terminal; it is an event of love composed and decomposed according to exactly the same, profoundly illogical, profoundly *lawless*, movement as the movement of lines moving "outward" and "back" both sequentially *and* simultaneously, an absolute declaration of unending love and the declaration of love's finitude.

It is this doubling as *sensible* experience, its occurrence as simultaneous and plural *sensation* that might—to recall Alain Badiou again—be described as a performance of poetic thought that is also a "singularity of a thought [that cannot] be replaced by the thinking of this thought."[13]

As a poet, this is what matters to me. As a critic, the neat fit between the movement of form and a paraphrasable lyric content (between the poetic line and love as both infinite and always-already terminal) is vaguely satisfying, even *homely*. Yet, as a poet, it is the way Estes consistently, inventively deploys the line-break (a variant of what Derrida would name as the *hymen*) as both the necessary condition of and a menace to the *heimlich*, the self as a readerly perspective in which poetic meaning cannot be schematized as anything other than an affective event and, thus, as a form of *love*, that I find so unthinkably brilliant.

This is what one feels so often in Estes's poems, but perhaps it is most explicit in "Paramour," from *Chez Nous*.

An adverb by way of
love, what's par for
l'amour is par
for the course. Say. . . .[14]

Estes is here preoccupied by language, and by a language both as and of love. These first lines unpick the etymology of the poem's title, "Paramour," that English noun that began life as an adverbial phrase in Old French, *par amour*, but its religious, idiomatic, and romantic variants also lingered on. *Trésor de la Langue Française*, for example, directs us to Simone Weil—"*La création est un acte d'amour et elle est perpétuelle. À chaque instant notre existence est amour de Dieu pour nous. . . . C'est Dieu qui par amour se retire de nous afin que nous puissions l'aimer*"[15]—as well as to the proverb: *tout par amour, rien par force*.

Yet something else is going on. In its original adverbial usage, "par amour" is akin to "with love," the intention of the verb is signified as that which is done out of love. In these lines, however, both line-break and pun insist on the experience of love as passage, as digression, remembering the connotations of "paramour" in English as *transgression*. "What's par for / *l'amour* is par / for the course" writes Estes, and we hear Shakespeare's Lysander declaiming "the course of true love never did run smooth." We might also hear Thom Gunn and his *Passages of Joy*, and although such a connotation might seem tenuous, one notes that Gunn's book opens with his poem "Elegy" and with "the terror / of leaving life,"[16] that terror at which Estes will arrive later in this poem.

Yet to pay attention to the first line-break of "Paramour" one finds "An adverb by way of . . . ," a "way" that falls off into the white space of the page before being filled with "love" and a "love" that is unexpected enough to be *revealed* by the advent of the subsequent line. Of course, there is a sense in English in which "by way of" might signify both the expression and the substitution of the noun to which it is appended. I might give you something, for example, "by way of an apology," but here "by way of" also harbors the structuration of the metaphor, the substitution of vehicle for tenor: I will give you something, and it will take the place of the apology I cannot truly *gift* to you because of the innate alterity of language; its inability to *be* the thing it signifies.

Both "by way of" as substitute and as detour are some way from the original signification of *par amour*. Or are they? Must such "amour" inevitably be both metaphor and *trial*? These are concerns that seem to me to play out through the rest of "Paramour," but such a "prismatic subdivision of the Idea"[17]—to cite Mallarmé's oft-cited postrationalization of poetic spatiality—is precisely what Estes's initial line-break performs. By the simple act of breaking the line, Estes strips the noun (love) from the adverbial phrase, insisting on the resonance of the *praxis* that constitutes either *par amour* or paramour. The blank page, the line-break, intervenes within the poem to institute a lyric event, a form of poetic emphasis on "by way of" as practice, that will congeal with how what follows— namely *l'amour*—is both read and *felt*.

Why is this of interest? Why is it so captivating? Not because a discourse might be constructed in which the problematization of love as event and as a process of language, instituted by this first line-break, can be read as that which unfolds throughout the rest of "Paramour" (though that is certainly a possibility). Rather, what is so powerful about this particular line-break is how it is deployed as an event of complicity, an event in which the reader's feelings are so acutely necessitated as a condition for the felt performance of the poem. It is an example of the poetic as *sensible* thinking.

> . . . Say
> you're out for dinner one evening
> with Yves, and you think of
> the phrase *evening*
> *of life*. Who doesn't want
> to be called something
> other than the name
> we're given: the cow we call
> *boeuf* or *beef* when eaten, the house
> when it's lived in,
> *home,* and the one we
> go home with, *love.*[18]

Note the terminal words of each line of this passage that meditates on being "called something / other." Note how the line-break imbues that "Say" with an emphasis, completely unlike its usually diminutive weight in the idiom it appears within; note how this same unusual level of stress is placed on "call." From a different perspective, note how thought ("truth") is set-up and undermined as it falls ("think of / the phrase") into mere idiom ("the phrase *evening* / *of life*"), and how *thought* and *desire* ("Who doesn't want / to be called") must both collapse into language.

I would suggest that, thanks to these *particular* line-breaks, "you think of" must always be felt as at least partially unassimilable with a particular referent ("the phrase *evening* / *of life*") and must always also maintain itself as the pure act of thinking *without* referent; it is a kind of thought both without the particularity of thinking a certain phrase and simultaneously as a thinking of "the phrase *evening* / *of life*." In the same way, pure desire ("who doesn't want") and desire as loss or lack ("who does not want") maintain themselves—thanks to the line-break that intervenes—both as a condition of and independent of the desire "to be called something," which must be felt as both the desire to be called something and the desire to be called something else ("to be called something / other").

At the risk of gratuitousness: "the cow we call" is still named as, and only as, "cow," even as it becomes *boeuf*; "home" and "house" maintain themselves simultaneously: the *feeling* of both are registered and must continue to resonate. Thus our own interiority—

that which we have eaten, those buildings we inhabit—coexists with a certain exteriority: the house, the cow, the name that is also simultaneously thought *and* desired. Here, as so often in Estes's work, the poem performs a beautifully unsettling performance of incessant *doubling*, a deployment of the line-break as a fugue-like conjunction in which what is presented is *re-presented* as other, and in which the poem occurs as this very process, this *praxis*, which the reader must go "by way of," constructing the poem as event by the act of the reader's *complicity*, rather than witnessing something that might warrant the term "mimesis."

> Lysippus, the Greek
> sculptor, used to say
> that his predecessors made men
> as they really were, but he made them as
> they appeared to be, just as Picasso
> replied to those who claimed Stein
> did not look like the portrait
> he made: *she will.* What makes
> the wine the wine, is it the grape
> or the *terroir*, terror or
> terrain?[19]

As Estes's line-breaks necessitate an experience of her poems as performative rather than mimetic, so Estes recalls here the odd image of the portrait and the sitter who *will come* to resemble her own representation. Yet it also seems that this portrait that comes *before* the sitter is exactly what readers are asked to confront (and to be complicit in) when they are faced with the line-break that occurs after "*terroir*, terror or."

At first glance, "terror" is a *faux ami* of "*terroir*," a deeply etymological mis-hearing (invoking the Latin *terra*, earth, and *terrere*, to frighten or make *tremble*), but it might also be read as something else. *Terroir*, in French, has its contemporaneous meaning of an ensemble of agricultural grounds. Yet there is also a secondary, more uncommon meaning of "territory" or "dominion," not altogether unrelated to the more abstract usage, the emotional evocation, with which it simultaneously designates, in France, a national treasure, a heartland, and maintains the sense of *une certaine fierté*. Such *fierté*, such pride, is not unrelated to *la Terreur*, The Terror, as one of the founding myths of the French Republic. Regardless, *terroir* as "domain" or "dominion" also, and emphatically, contains a certain notion of terror, as national and nationalist mythologies inevitably sow terror somewhere, most often in the "other."

If these are the discursive implications of the lines cited above, what is so much more interesting is how this "or" terminates within the intervention of a space that is infinite to the extent it lacks a referent, to the extent it is merely "an image of itself."[20] What is amazing is how this deftly deployed line-break sows the feeling of *terror* into the subsequent *terrain*, maintaining such terror even as the reader is led back to sturdy ground. More than this, though, is how wonderfully succinct this "or /" embodies the "or" of the line-break: not as the division between two options of which one must decide, but as a kind of "or" that undoes the possibility of judicial discourse, an "or" that is always-already the most radical (and, to recall Badiou, the most *lawless*) "and."

> . . . What's uncanny,
> *unheimlich,* in German is not
> *heimlich,* secret, and certainly not *heim,*
> home, which means home can't be
> where the heart is but the Hôtel
> Tassel in Brussels, whose staircases
> turn and let down their lips
> to meet you, whips unfurling
> like vines. Freud said we'll know
> the uncanny when surprised
> by some *heimlich,* some fear or
> desire we've repressed
> come home. . . .[21]

If in "Paramour" home is the house as "lived in," the place we take our *love*, he or she who "we / go home with," here—in "On Yellowed Velvet"—the home "can't be / where the heart is." Rather, it is the "Hôtel / Tassel in Brussels."

In one sense, this might be a perfect example of what Hollander called *anagnorisis*. In this model, the reader is told that the "home" is not the "lived in" home of the popular imagination ("where the heart is"), but is a Hôtel, the figuration of flux. After the reader moves to the next line, she realizes it is a *specific* hotel, recognizing and readjusting herself to the "correct" reading while maintaining the amplified evocation of this specific place as one of flux. And yet this would be to ignore what the line-break, the intervention of the page, enacts.

The home is not simply *not* "where the heart is" but it is the *hôtel*. "Before" it is the Hôtel Tassel, it is the *hôtel* as, in its Old French precedent, *ostel*, as "lodging." Yet the violence with which the page intervenes, paring the line to size, makes one wonder if it is not also the *hôte*, that odd French word that can mean both "host" and "guest," and thus so often both subject *and* object. It is not that this feeling of the home stripped down to lodging is an ancillary gesture that the space of the line-break offers up as a secondary connotation, as a supplement to what Derrida warns would be the mere "lexical richness" of the signifier. Rather the line-break intervenes as permanence, making the home always-already *felt* as both hostel and guest, lodger and lodging; just as it becomes, and simultaneously is, the "Hôtel Tassel."

Further, as Estes recalls the Freudian *unheimlich*, this passage, this particular line-break, also brings to mind Freud's *Civilization and Its Discontents*, in which he writes:

At the height of being in love the boundary between ego and object threatens to melt away. Against all the evidence of his senses, a man who is in love declares that "I" and "you" are one, and is prepared to behave as if it were a fact. . . . Pathology has made us acquainted with a great number of states in which the boundary lines between the ego and the external world become uncertain or in which they are actually drawn incorrectly.[22]

The effacement of the division between subject ("ego") and object is also the effacement of what Julia Kristeva has called the "precondition . . . of propositionality,"[23] and is—as Freud points out—what we might also know as either psychosis or *love*.

Estes's "home" as host and guest, as lodging and the experience of the lodger, as—thanks to the intervention of the line-break— both *subject* and *object* is also a paradigm for what one might see as her deployment of the line-break as a quietly radical disruption of the unity of the lyric "I" and of what we might call, rather than "object," the *subject of representation*. The line-break is operative of a collapse of syntactic temporality, a making simultaneous of the Hôtel as noun (Hôtel, lodging, etc.) and as proper noun (Hôtel Tassel), as both Idea and *thing*. It is a doubling of the word as referential object and the grammatical objectification of subjective experience. Fundamentally, Estes's line-break undoes the opposition between subject and object, between lyric "I" and the object, or referent, of the poem by reconstituting such objects as events of the reader's subjective, deeply felt complicity.

The artist and poet Carl Andre once wrote that "the point of art is participation, by the artist in his work of making the artwork, by the observer in his work of making the artwork a part of his consciousness."[24] The reason, I believe, that I go back so often to Angie Estes's poems as exemplary instances of the lyric line-break, and why I so often hand them out to students, is because her deployment of the line-break is so often the construction of the poem, the poetic event, as precisely an emphatic form of *participation*. Her work offers up instance after instance in which the line-break is deployed as an invitation, and exaltation, for the reader's participation, their complicity, in producing the poem itself.

Such line-breaks, as I have suggested above, undo the Aristotelian tenet of an opposition between "and" and "or," constructing the poem as a certain kind of *unheimlich* home. They produce the poem—to return to "Paramour"—as a "way of / love" that dissolves the distinction between subject (reader) and object (poem), by producing the latter as an *effect* of the former, and—thanks to the affective potency of Estes's line-breaks—rendering the reader's affect as both complicity in and condition of the poem. At their most radical, Estes's line-breaks render the poem as *sensible* thought, as a sequence of "or"s that are also "and"s that, in the very *lawlessness* of the syntax this constructs, can only be felt as thought and as the profound, and profoundly successful, event of a language that demands be lived.

Notes

1. Angie Estes. *Chez Nous* (Oberlin: Oberlin College Press, 2005), 15.

2. Alain Badiou. *Handbook of Inaesthetics*, trans. Alberto Toscado (Stanford: Stanford University Press, 2005), 17.

3. Ibid.

4. Ibid., 19.

5. Ibid., 27.

6. Angie Estes. *Tryst* (Oberlin: Oberlin College Press, 2009), 7.

7. John Milton. *Paradise Lost* (Oxford: Oxford University Press, 2008), 85.

8. Jonathan Culler. *Structuralist Poetics* (London: Routledge, 2002), 216.

9. John Hollander. "'Sense Variously Drawn Out': Some Observations on English Enjambment." In *Literary Theory and Structure*, ed. Frank Brady et al. (London: Yale University Press, 1973), 207.

10. Jacques Derrida. *Dissemination*, trans. Barbara Johnson (London: Continuum, 2004), 229.

11. Estes, *Tryst*, 7–8.

12. Theodor W. Adorno. *Negative Dialectics*, trans. E. B. Ashton (London: Routledge, 1990), 33.

13. Badiou, 27.

14. Estes, *Chez Nous*, 3.

15. Simone Weil. *La Pesanteur et la grâce* (Paris: Pocket, 1993), 42.

16. Thom Gunn. *The Passages of Joy* (London: Faber, 2010), 9.

17. Stephane Mallarmé. *Un Coup de Dés Jamais n'Abolira le Hasard* (Paris: La Nouvelle Revue Française, 1914), 1.

18. Estes, *Chez Nous*, 3.

19. Estes, *Chez Nous*, 3.

20. Ibid.

21. Estes, *Chez Nous*, 62.

22. Sigmund Freud. "Civilisation and its Discontents." In *The Standard Edition of the Complete Psychological Works of Sigmund Freud: Volume XXI*, ed. James Strachey (London: Vintage, 2001), 66.

23. Julia Kristeva. *Revolution in Poetic Language*, trans. Margaret Walker (New York: Columbia University Press, 1984), 43.

24. Carl Andre. "A Note on Participation (1968)." In *Cuts: Texts 1959–2004*, ed. James Meyer (Cambridge: MIT Press, 2005), 30.

LEE UPTON

On Angie Estes
An Erotics of Italics

Angie Estes draws attention both to the shapeliness of lines and to
the shapeliness of individual letters as her poems move between
discrete particulars and large structures of reference. She frequently
manipulates scale in her poetry: from stag heads to constellations, a
cup of espresso and a bridge, scrapple and the Via Sacra. "I think of
the poem as one of those things in the world that is filled with 'di-
vine details,' and the poem is an arranged place," she told an inter-
viewer.[1] Such attention to "divine details" in the midst of more
capacious arrangements and competing perspectives animates her
work: an elephant's weight approximates that of a blue whale's
tongue; "What is called / a 'French kiss' in the English-speaking //
world is called an 'English kiss' / in France";[2] Dali invented a jacket
"studded with shot glasses / filled with crème de menthe."[3] Espe-
cially at the close of her poems the letters that make up words prove
mobile and malleable, generating new implications: *wisteria* leads to
hysteria, posse to *possess.* From a close focus on the materials of her
art—the alphabet itself—Estes may shift abruptly to soaring ab-
stractions, the flying buttresses of spiritually focused images, and a
range of quotations, languages, and textual references that braid
through her work.

"[T]o understand how the words of / the dead go on speaking,"[4]
Estes keeps in motion quotations from multiple sources across time
periods. Conventionally, a quotation may serve primarily as a bor-
rowed authority or as evidence. In Estes's poems quotations enliven
and stretch expressive potential to create an arching or vault-like
effect. Rather than blending quotation marks into the body of the
poem, or relying exclusively on notes, Estes foregrounds the tex-
tured surfaces that italics create. The quoted portions within her
work constitute an almost ziggurat-like layering that may continu-
ally challenge our sense of certainty or direction. Sentences mean-
der through borrowed references that are visually and emphatically
made apparent by italics.

The choice of italics to designate quotations, although unsurprising, isn't an inevitable one. The problem of acknowledging and integrating quoted material frustrated a poet with whom Estes is often compared. In "A Note on the Notes" Marianne Moore makes clear the dilemma:

> A willingness to satisfy contradictory objections to one's manner of writing might turn one's work into the donkey that finally found itself being carried by its masters, since some readers suggest that quotation-marks are disruptive of pleasant progress; others, that notes to what should be complete are a pedantry or evidence of an insufficiently realized task. But since in anything I have written, there have been lines in which the chief interest is borrowed, and I have not yet been able to outgrow this hybrid method of composition, acknowledgments seem only honest.[5]

"This hybrid method of composition" links Moore and Estes; both arrange borrowed materials that may at first glance appear only tentatively related to their poems' subjects. For her part, Moore relies on quotation marks and notes to acknowledge quotations. Estes uses notes in her books' closing pages but uses italics prominently in her poems. By my count, in Estes's first collection, *The Uses of Passion*, italics are located in the body of thirteen of the collection's forty poems. In her second collection, *Voice-Over*, only one poem in the entire collection appears without italics: "*Musique d'Ameublement*," and the title itself is in italics. In her third collection, *Chez Nous*, all poems include italics except for a single section of "Ensemble"; notably, that poem, "The House of Worth," is a translation of the previous poem (Paul Reboux's advertisement) that is cast entirely in italics. In her next two collections, *Tryst* and *Echantée*, every poem contains italics.

Beyond the conventional ways that italic font may designate titles, quotations, emphasis, or non-English words, Estes's choice of italics, tracking across her poems, not only makes visually emphatic the fact that many of her poems owe part of their material to more than one language, more than one speaker, or more than one text but also, when used repeatedly, draw attention to her aesthetic. Italic font demarcates a momentary moving away from the speaker/author as point of origin for the poem and highlights the role of the author as one who gathers and arranges material from other sites.

Italics measure space—between the author's original words and borrowed words, including non-English words, underscoring connections between the living and the nonliving as well as between time periods, cultures, and genres as each occupies the same poem and influences our understanding.

We may visualize italic font through a range of metaphors: italics resemble a ribbon, a scrolling, an embroidery. Italics lean and slip away from the straight, as if to mark a seam, a pull at nonitalicized words, creating additional surface figuration. Estes makes clear that the particular visual form of italics attracts her as an indication of the human wish to ornament, to create graceful and inviting forms. Sloping, interrupting nonitalicized font, italics reinforce Estes's exdents and indents, her manipulation of white space, to suggest suspension, hovering actions between categories.

The decorative, often associated culturally with women and presumed in many instances to be unauthoritative and trifling, is in Estes's poetry cast as life-affirming, a brimming-over that creates beauty and a gloss on beauty, overturning assumptions of value. Estes's clear pleasure in ornamentation and figuration that borders on excess connects her with Wallace Stevens. Like Stevens she satisfies a desire to burnish or elaborately mark experience through an aesthetic that calls attention to its own materials. She writes about rejecting a "clean" upright font in "*Sans Serif*":

> It's the opposite of
> Baroque, so I want
> none of it—clean
> and spare, like Cassius
> it has that lean
> and hungry look. . . .

In the poem's closing lines, she describes opera cake, an opulent dessert. The filigree of italics hangs after the dash: "its name is scrolled / in glaze across the top—*l'opéra* / finished with a lick / of gold leaf."[6] The italics serve as ornament, a "glazing," and as such an enhancement of pleasure.

The origins of italics are disputed. In *The Oxford English Dictionary* italics are defined as "the species of printing type introduced by Aldus Manutius of Venice, in which the letters, instead of being erect as in Roman, slope towards the right; first used in an edition of Virgil, published in 1501 and dedicated to Italy." Simon Garfield in *Just My Type* notes: "It is widely believed that the inspiration [for italic font] stemmed from the hand of Niccolo Niccoli, a contemporary Venetian who used a slanted style when he wished to write faster or express dynamism. However, punchsetters in Florence also subsequently placed a claim."[7]

If the inspiration for italics is in some dispute, that uncertainty seems of a piece with Estes's focus on what escapes certainty and visibility in her own work. In *Chez Nous* a speaker referencing a particular font, "Rage Italic," asks "is there a font / for what takes place // offstage?"[8] Italic font is summoned in the poem as a means to imagine a notation for what we can't see or for what is "ghosted," given that italics conventionally denote the "foreign" or statements that may be gathered from those who are absent. The poem continues:

> . . .When it is emphatic,
> in a foreign language, or when
>
> it has an independent function within
> the main text, *the sentence is printed*
>
> *in italics*, but like the roulette wheel
> in Reno, the truth is
>
> what it turns out
> to be, and belief
>
> a bet we place,
> like baseball cards clipped
>
> with clothespins to the spokes
> of our bikes, the patter
>
> of birds in a stone
> bath. *Pater Noster*,
>
> give us a set, one size, one
> face of, say, *rage*
>
> *italic*, favorite font
> of the gods.[9]

Rage italic, designed by Ron Zwingelberg in 1984, is "a casual brush script with the appearance of pen on parchment."[10] It is likely that an accent on "rage" attracted Estes as the word resonates throughout the poem and applies to her meditations on mortality, chance, and belief. If one of the specific functions of italics is to earmark a sentence "when // it has an independent function within / the main text," then the gods referenced in the poem as ruling cruelly and absolutely are the only presences gifted with an "independent function." The rest of us are dependent and gamble on belief. Italics here mark intractable contrasts in power.

If, as Estes claims, "the job of the poem is to heighten our experience of our experience in some way,"[11] attention to the forms of individual letters of the alphabet may lead to heightened sensory awareness. In "Script" the patterns of letters in calligraphy take on metaphoric resemblances: flags, pasta, chain links, stems, a knot, a stitch, "the line / from a fly rod," a fish hook.[12] Her attention to script is further evident in the same collection in her homage to Nijinsky, "Here Lightning Has Been":

> . . . In his diary,
> Nijinsky wrote that he had
> invented a fountain pen
> called God: *Handwriting*
> *is a beautiful thing,*
> *and therefore it must be*
> *preserved.*[13]

Estes links a photograph of the great dancer in mid-leap to the volatility of his hand moving across the page as he writes. The way letters are formed conveys kinetics, an aesthetic of expressive movement. She again quotes Nijinsky:

> *I know that if I show*
> *my handwriting to someone who can*
> *read the future, he will say*
> *that this man is extraordinary,*
> *for his handwriting*
> *jumps.*[14]

Estes's selections from *The Diary of Vaslav Nijinsky* reinforce, through italicized quotations, her preoccupation with the shapeliness of letters. She reconfirms that script, referred to as handwritten in this poem, or the calligraphy in other poems, or the digitized font that reappears in her own collections, should be appreciated as a feature of art that merits imaginative attention.

If we turn again to "Rage Italic," we can see that Estes imagines a font balanced on seemingly irreconcilable categories: presence and absence:

> . . . From Old French, *font*
> follows *fondre*, to melt
>
> to cast, to found, to blend
> or vanish. *What is here*
>
> *and not?* The lost
> and found, what's
>
> italicized, *beurre Normande*,
> what we never
>
> mention, whatever will melt
> in your mouth.[15]

By associating the font with butter (*buerre Normandie*), Estes may in turn be drawing from one of her earliest realizations about aesthetic discrimination. In the interview referenced earlier, Estes calls attention repeatedly to "divine detail," a phrase used by the interviewer: "For as long as I can remember I've had a very strong sense of what you term 'divine detail' in the world—beginning perhaps with my realization that the butter my grandmother made in the mountains of Virginia tasted incredibly different than the store-bought butter I ate at home in suburban Maryland."[16] At the close of "Rage Italic" italics are summoned to suggest what may physically disappear but may be remembered—what "will melt" but is not actually lost, for memory secures what is otherwise unavailable. In the same interview Estes quotes, with admiration, Jeanette Winterson's words: "Every work of art is an attempt to bring into being the object of loss." In Estes's poetry the particulars of her own personal experience are summoned in the midst of her representations of artistic works that resonate with depictions of loss.

In conversation with Lauren Berlant, Lee Edelman in *Sex, or the*

Unbearable presents loss as its assumed opposite, presence, in a way that resonates with Estes's meditations:

> Loss is what, in the object-relation, it's impossible to lose; it's what you're left with when an object changes its place or changes its state. Even change for the better, even gain involves such loss, where loss is not merely an emptiness but something more dimensional, something that fills the vacated space that's left by what used to be there. Loss, in such a context, may be a name for what survives. In the place of what one had before, loss remains to measure the space or distance relation requires.[17]

Loss is never quite "lost" in Estes's poems, just as the poem "melts" in Robert Frost's famous formulation ("like a piece of ice on a hot stove the poem must ride on its own melting"). As such, italics may signal space in which we're reminded of absent voices or of difference itself. We might turn once again to Marianne Moore to contemplate how loss works as a shadow presence in Estes's poetry and conditions the experiences she creates in her poems. Moore's famous quotation "Omissions are not accidents" refers to her severe editing of her poems during her late career. The quotation is most often cited in reference to Moore's poem "Poetry," from which she cut over two dozen lines in a late version. In some ways Moore's severe cutting was a brilliant career move for "Poetry," securing the poem's prominence as a locus for discussion. If we know differing versions of Moore's "Poetry," we may find it difficult to read her final version without recalling its far longer predecessor. The well-known revised poem in turn might illustrate the quotation from Henry James that Estes draws into "Colors Are Not True" in *Enchantée*.

> Even when clouds gray the sky
> on a winter day in Paris, there is
> as Henry James said, *a presence*
> *in what is missing. . . .*[18]

In Estes's poems a sense of the lost or the absent shadows the lines. The open-work through white spaces, the steep drops between levels of diction and historical ranges of reference, and the way italics occupy many lines and lean toward the margin—as if to move off the page—alert us to "*a presence in what is missing.*" Her poems' frequent reach toward what her readers often consider to be a near-Baroque style of elaboration remains contingent on her perception of experience as inherently contoured by the intricacy of memories, and the outsized yearning for meaning that has its foundation in her early experiences as they may be revisited and reinterpreted. That is, a suggestion of loss is presented repeatedly, as immediate personal experience inflects her vaulting references to wide-ranging aesthetic experience. Significantly, Estes counts the Baptist church of her childhood as a primary inspiration:

> [T]he hymns, the prayers, the communion, the scripture, the hellfire and damnation sermons, and the revivals: the insistent belief in metaphor and symbol and language, and the insistent conviction that there is a connection between this world and some "other." All of this, too, made clear that the "divine details"—of a life, of the world, of language—were in fact a means of transport or, more precisely, that to partake of those "divine details" was to be already in the process of transport and translation.[19]

For Estes, linguistic performances create "transport," stretching the body's capacities. She renders even individual letters as vulnerable bodies, as in "Ars Poetica" in *Enchantée*: "I once dreamed a word entirely / Baroque: a serpentine line of letters leaning / with the flourish of each touching the shoulder / of another so that one breath at the word's / beginning made them all collapse."[20] Language, figured as a body of sorts, exerts control over other bodies. In "Recall" she quotes the philosopher Gaston Bachelard to insist that even while reading silently we are physically changed and must respond: "Bachelard recalls how / the French baritone said it is impossible // to think the vowel sound *ah* without / tensing, tightening the vocal chords: *we read* ah / *and the voice is ready to sing.*"[21] In "Hail to Thee," (the comma is part of the title), St. Augustine's words, italicized, close the poem: "*When you read these words, / I speak, and your voice / is mine.*"[22] While the original writer is lost to us, the writer's words exert their presence and seemingly "inhabit" the reader.

"But since when / is a sentence ever innocent?" Estes asks in "Revision."[23] If we look at the opening poem in her first book, a poem that italicizes the title of a nonexistent poem, a projected poem of the imagination, we can see how eroticism may underlie the work she attributes to the attention her creative process requires. Although in the first stanza the title of the wished-for poem is printed without quotation marks, when the poem arrives its title comes clothed in italics. "A Poem Called Lost at Sea" concludes:

> The irony of the poem would be that no one would ever
> cry out "Land ho!" because, of course,
> We were lost at sea, tacking carelessly
> Across the hips of the ocean, and it was night,
> And as in all good poems, in the depths lurked
>
> Hidden meaning. One day, sun-rotted, the sails
> Would mercifully unzip, and the naked lines of a poem
> Called *Lost at Sea* could finally suggest
> What happened: How your tongue stuck inside me like an oar,
> How you and your boat kept turning, turning, turning.[24]

Unabashedly erotic, "Lost at Sea" recounts a desire to create a poem sufficiently able to "suggest" what happens between lovers. The final actions are explicit in their references to the sexualized body and may also refer to the "tongue" of other voices and other languages, those italicized entities that will increasingly constitute parts of Estes's poems in her subsequent collections.

In her fourth collection, Estes imagines the messages lovers in Venice left for one another—initially messages without words, only physical gestures:

> *. . . Touch your hair*
> *if you're going to the Ridotto. Nod*
> *or shake your head*
> *to tell me whether you plan to*
> *go to the piazza,* Venetian
> lovers once wrote in secret
> notes that from the air
> could be mistaken
> for ruins along the canal where
> they met: runes arching their backs
> against the sea. Your plane taxis
> out to the runway; in a moment it will
> lift as you have so many times
> beneath me.[25]

Ascending—one of the primary repeated actions in many of her poems in terms of spiritual or aesthetic concerns—is here captured in terms of erotics and is linked to "secret / notes." After conjuring the distant past, the speaker turns to a beloved's departure or arrival and simultaneously summons a form of erotic power. The poem ends with images of motion, a kinetics of beauty like that which underlies so much of her work, including her attention to fonts as she perceives individual letters as shaped and reshaped by artistic attention.

Tellingly, what Estes terms "bodily engagement" or "the bodies / of . . . letters" preoccupies her poem "Love Letters" in *Tryst*. Here the actions of ascending and descending so frequently enacted in her poems appear in her attention to calligraphy and ornate script:

> Fish swim atop letter Ts, shafts of wheat
> spring up along or as the shanks
> of M and N, and hearts bloom
> out of Ds like lamb chop sleeves
> in the script of the fifteenth-century
> scribe Ricardus Franciscus.[26]

Estes invites us to appreciate the alphabet not only in the form of ornate calligraphy but by focusing on the continuing potential for transformation in the varied shapes of the alphabet. For her, the letters that comprise a written language in physical form are expressions of creative radiance. As such, she sets in motion what might be called "visionary fragment[s]" as Elaine Scarry uses the phrase in *On Beauty and Being Just*:

> [B]eauty is for the beholder lifesaving or life-restoring—a visionary fragment of sturdy ground. . . . The thing perceived, the beautiful object, has conferred on it by the beholder a surfeit of aliveness; even if it is inanimate, it comes to be accorded a fragility and consequent level of protection normally reserved for the animate. . . .[27]

The visual imprints of italics as designating emphasis and difference contribute to the way Estes's poems constellate meaning and summon beauty. Her poems may remind readers of an illuminated manuscript as her resonant lines highlight ornate images of aspiration and wonder. Repeatedly, she pays attention to the most fine-grained elements by which meaning is made, including "the way a period haunts / a sentence."[28] Or the way "we are the hammocks / in which the commas swing."[29] Or the way the slope of a font carries fresh meaning as she advocates for and defends devoted attentiveness to even the minute particulars of her art.

Notes

1. Angie Estes, interview with Karen Rigby. "Means of Transport, Medieval Mind: Dialogue with Angie Estes." This volume, p. 69.
2. Angie Estes. *Tryst* (Oberlin: Oberlin College Press, 2009), 16.
3. Angie Estes. *Enchantée* (Oberlin: Oberlin College Press, 2013), 44.
4. Estes, *Enchantée*, 55.
5. Marianne Moore. "Marianne Moore's Notes." *The Poems of Marianne Moore*, ed. Grace Schulman (New York: Viking, 2003), 375.
6. Angie Estes. "*Sans Serif*," from *Chez Nous* (Oberlin: Oberlin College Press, 2005), 28.
7. Simon Garfield. *Just My Type: A Book About Fonts* (New York: Random House, 2011), 80.
8. Angie Estes. "Rage Italic," from *Chez Nous*, 41.
9. Ibid., 41–42.
10. Identifont.com. Available at http://www.identifont.com/show?34W
11. Estes, "Means of Transport, Medieval Mind: Dialogue with Angie Estes." This volume, p. 73.
12. Estes, *Tryst*, 22.
13. Estes, *Tryst*, 23.
14. Ibid., 24.
15. Estes, *Chez Nous*, 43.
16. Estes, "Means of Transport." This volume, p. 67.
17. Lee Edelman and Lauren Berlant. *Sex, or the Unbearable* (Durham: Duke University Press, 2014), 47.
18. Estes, *Enchantée*, 10.
19. Estes, "Means of Transport."
20. Estes, *Enchantée*, 56.
21. Estes, *Enchantée*, 64.
22. Estes, *Enchantée*, 50.
23. Estes, *Enchantée*, 58.
24. Angie Estes. *The Uses of Passion* (Salt Lake City: Gibbs-Smith, 1995), 2.
25. Estes, *Tryst*, 8.
26. Estes, *Tryst*, 5.
27. Elaine Scarry. *On Beauty and Being Just* (Princeton: Princeton University Press, 1999), 89.
28. Estes, *Tryst*, 26.
29. Angie Estes. *Voice-Over* (Oberlin: Oberlin College Press, 2002), 16.

NANCY KUHL

On Angie Estes's *Chez Nous*

The arresting cover image on *Chez Nous* points to key elements
within in a way few book covers do. An elegant photograph of
Peggy Guggenheim at the window of Kay Sage's Paris apartment,
circa 1940, the cover image, like Estes's poems, considers the many
layers of perception and reveals the complex dynamics of space and
vision. We see Guggenheim, wearing a dress made partially of cel-
lophane, standing before a window that reveals a hazy and slightly
obscured view of Notre Dame. There is, at once, a feeling of famil-
iarity and a sense of foreignness; the tension between interior and
exterior, intimate and public is palpable. In Angie Estes's poems,
the sometimes confused and sometimes conflicted public and pri-
vate meanings of individual words are both revealed and hidden—
like Peggy Guggenheim's body under the contradictory materials
of her dress, the substantial fabric and translucent cellophane.
Throughout *Chez Nous,* Estes is interested in the ways language
maps both interior and exterior landscapes, exposing contours and
corners, pathways and distances. And the distances she travels with
regard to subject are nothing short of remarkable; in *Chez Nous* we
venture from Paris to Delphi to Rome, encountering Miles Davis
and Mae West, Marcus Aurelius and Pliny, to name only a few.
These poems mark the territories of both intellect and emotion—
often at once and with an attention to lyric and image that is strik-
ing and memorable. Take for instance "True Confessions," the first
poem in the collection. Like many of the poems in *Chez Nous*, it
includes clever word play that draws on both sound and meaning:
"glamour is its own / allure, thrashing and / flashing, a lure, a
spoon / as in spooning, as in *l'amour*."[1] It also introduces one of
Estes's central mediations (obsessions?), the sometimes curious ety-
mologies of common words, the layered meanings buried within
the familiar. "And the true / home of glamour, by which / I mean
of course the grammar / of glamour," Estes writes, "is Scotland /
because glamour is a Scottish variant / of grammar with its rustle
of moods / and desires."[2]

In just fifty-four lines, we hear the voices of Rita Hayworth and St. Augustine, visit the Scottish hills and Coney Island, and face the confusion of desire and contempt, sex and violence evident in the strange fact that a pin-up of Hayworth rode the atomic bomb tested at Bikini Atoll. Estes constructs poems by piling idea on top of idea, image on top of image, meaning on top of meaning, creating elaborate and complex structures—dwellings, as it were. *"And indeed / if we consider this beautiful / machine of the world, /* Palladio wrote, so much needs / oiling," Estes writes in the book's title poem, "the porch swing / of the chickadee's song, the mourning / dove flung up like the window's / wooden sash, the word *rudbeckia.* // And isn't news / rude, the way it beckons? *Le corps* becomes a copse, someone's / opus, but we can't imagine / whose because *chez nous* / the peonies dress for dinner / like grizzlies // in their pungent fuchsia coats."[3]

With her method of accumulation Estes suggests that it might be impossible to express anything in more direct terms; the surprising precision of word and image in these poems standing in sharp contrast with language's inevitable inexactness seems to argue that the idea of creating an authentic representation of image, idea, or experience out of language without employing such layers is not possible. "What's uncanny," Estes writes in "On Yellowed Velvet," "unheimlich, in German is not / heimlich, secret, and certainly not heim, / home, which means home can't be / where the heart is but the Hôtel / Tassel in Brussels, whose staircases / turn and let down their lips / to meet you, whips unfurling / like vines."[4] Angie Estes is a poet who puts words and phrases through their paces, always calling attention to the way language—any language—can mask its own roots and gather meanings around itself. "Let words / be the Montmorency cherries I bought / at market," Estes writes in "Palinode," "because the woman pronounced them / *Mount Mercy*, let them be the tumult / of memory, mute."[5] In "Kind of Blue," she writes "What if / you paused for a minuet // instead of a minute? The dark / might sky, the blue might // star, the always / could open, the close // might earth."[6] For Estes, word play is serious business, but she is not without a sense of humor and her poems are often rich with wit. "The woods fill / with accent trees or, if / you prefer, eccentricities,"[7] she writes in one poem, and in another: "decide whether you'd rather / remember spending hours / next to the sea, against / the sea, or in ecstasy."[8] That language, even in one's native tongue, both unites and isolates us is everywhere evident in

Chez Nous. Estes's poems are marked with a sense of the pervasive foreignness of language and with the curiosities and imaginative possibilities of bilingualism. In "A History of Reality," Estes writes: "Taken literally the shore would be / *littoral* and the ocean its Latin / lover *litura*, erasure or / correction, clearing the beach / like a windshield with its big / glassy hands."[9] And in "Portrait," a poem that makes much of Picasso's portrait of Gertrude Stein, a writer and thinker who acts as a kind of touchstone for Estes, "The irises keep opening // into *fleur-de-lis*, and *le désir* // and *les idées* come back / each April as *des iridées*."[10] Angie Estes is interested in the way meaning inhabits language, the way we who use, abuse, stretch, and sometimes transform it also inhabit language, but perhaps more importantly, she is interested in the ways language and meaning, and by extension poetry, inhabit and transform us. In *Chez Nous*, language is a dwelling place but not really a comfortable home; it is an uncertain site, an untrustworthy foundation on which, nevertheless, an incredible and extravagant structure is built. The achievement and satisfaction of this fine book is Estes's constant lyrical reminder that it is a structure capable of holding all manner of joy and horror, humor and grief: "whether it's memory or loss / we're in need of most," the poet wonders, "to remember / the way home or forget / who we are when we get there."[11]

Notes

1. Angie Estes. *Chez Nous* (Oberlin: Oberlin College Press, 2005), 1.
2. Ibid., 1.
3. Ibid., 36–37.
4. Ibid., 62.
5. Ibid., 67.
6. Ibid., 14.
7. Ibid., 63.
8. Ibid., 30.
9. Ibid., 64.
10. Ibid., 9.
11. Ibid., 2.

KAREN RIGBY

Means of Transport, Medieval Mind

Dialogue with Angie Estes

KAREN RIGBY: Several of your poems concern words as visual artifacts, drawing from illuminated manuscripts or typography. How did you discover this reverence for beauty and workmanship, for the "divine detail?"

ANGIE ESTES: For as long as I can remember, I've had a very strong sense of what you term "divine detail" in the world—beginning perhaps with my realization that the butter my grandmother made in the mountains of Virginia tasted incredibly different than the store-bought butter I ate at home in suburban Maryland. And the ham. And the potatoes. In my Uncle Osie's chair factory, I watched unremarkable lengths of walnut turned on lathes to become the legs and rungs and backs of chairs, and I followed my Aunt Evelyn out in the dark at 5 a.m. to milk the cows in the muddy barn, then watched her pour the milk through a dish towel clothespinned over the top of the separator as the milk and cream went their separate ways. Those, too, tasted like things from another world, a world I could partake of by means of those things. Above all, my sense was always that there was a connection between who these people were, the lives they lived, and the "divine details" that made up those lives. But even though I experienced all of this and carried it inside me, I could never take it with me, transport it to and evoke those experiences in any other place.

And then there was the Baptist church—the hymns, the prayers, the communion, the scripture, the hellfire and damnation sermons, and the revivals: the insistent belief in metaphor and symbol and language, and the insistent conviction that there is a connection between this world and some "other." All of this, too, made clear that the "divine details"—of a life, of the world, of language—were in fact a means of transport or, more precisely, that to partake of those "divine details" was to be already in the process of transport and translation.

Much later I encountered Goethe and his belief that nature is the living visible garment of God, along with the British and American Romantics—especially Blake, with his inexhaustible attempts to make language and imagination and visual art into a more profound inhabitation of experience, and Emerson's essay "Nature," too, with its amazing image of the "transparent eyeball" one could become while out in nature, where the currents of the human and the universe could mingle and inform each other.

And I was enthralled by Emerson's disciples Dickinson and Melville, with their particular American modern slant on the relationship—not always a pleasant one—between the human and the "divine details" of nature and the universe. Ahab's invocation to "Hark ye yet again,—the little lower layer" because "All visible objects . . . are but as pasteboard masks," along with Rilke's notion that humans are "the bees of the invisible world" became especially significant for me.

All of this is by way of saying that by the time I encountered medieval writing, art, and architecture, I was primed to fall in love with it. For in a sense I'd been doing a kind of medieval "anagogical" thinking most of life—reading the details of this world in the light of some other world. And I love the whole medieval idea that the world is something that can be *read*. All of this really came together for me when I read the work of Abbot Suger, who placed gold and precious stones and *objets* in the chapel of St. Denis and wrote about how aesthetic pleasure and beauty could give rise to mystical ecstasy, how the light from these gems could transport him to "some strange region of the universe which neither exists entirely in the slime of the earth nor entirely in the purity of heaven," by means of which "by the grace of God, I can be transported from this inferior to that higher world in an anagogical manner."

KR: Has studying medieval works influenced your writing?

AE: Medieval thought, writing, art, and architecture were enormously important to my ideas about what a poem can be. For the medieval mind, everything bristles with meaning—nothing is static. And the active, engaged mind is the mind that can be, and is, transported. I think of a poem as one of those things in the world that is filled with "divine details," and the poem is an arranged place—like the golden chalices, rubies, emeralds, and stained-glass windows of Abbot Suger's chapel—where experience happens. And although this is in some ways a very modernist way of talking about art and poetry, it also has a long lineage, running back through Wallace Stevens and Dickinson—and at least back to medieval thinkers and writers. Flannery O'Connor, too, in her essays about writing fiction, talks about the importance of anagogical thinking.

And of course, the medieval delight in the things of the world, in "divine detail," is in itself an inexhaustible fascination for both reader and writer. Medieval authors and artists offer perhaps our greatest example of the human imagination in the constant act of reading and writing the world.

KR: Fra Angelico has inspired poems in both *Tryst* and *Voice-Over*. What draws you to his art?

AE: Yes, as I was just saying, I believe that a work of art—or a poem—must make an arrangement that creates an experience for a viewer or reader, that pulls the viewer into the work of art so that something happens to the viewer. This seems to me a central preoccupation of medieval thought and art, and Fra Angelico is a master of creating these visual arrangements that are powerful and involving experiences. In his frescoes at San Marco in *Firenze*, for example, the painting in each of the monk's cells invokes a moving meditation on a significant moment in the life of Christ but does so within the architectural context specific to each individual cell, thus invoking a kind of anagogical tension between past and present, human and divine, sacred and mundane. Likewise, at the top of the staircase leading up to the cells, Fra Angelico embraces the viewer with his *Annunciation*, the rainbow hues of the heavenly angel's wing glistening with the earthly silica Fra Angelico has mixed into his paint.

KR: Speaking of the medieval reminds me of the craft guilds, and of the path from apprentice to master. Any parallels with the current literary world, and whether a community of the like-minded is important?

AE: The teacher part of me says, ah, if only we *had* a kind of medieval craft guild for writing poems! One of the hardest things for apprentice writers to get is that it takes at least as long to learn what poems are and how to write them as it takes to learn what a chair is and how to craft a beautiful, useful one or as long as it takes to become a ballet dancer or a violinist or pianist. And it's a never-ending process. So yes, I think that both an apprenticeship with a poet and the company of the like-minded can be extremely important for a writer—as long as they're not mistaken for the real work of a poet, which is mostly long and solitary.

I myself never went to an MFA writing program—or took part in writing workshops—so my own sense of how one becomes a poet is a very traditional, pre-writing program one: poets read and read, study the work of other writers, pay attention to the world, and write. And a very large part of me agrees with Mallarmé when, in his essay "Art for All," he says, "Whatever is sacred, whatever is to remain sacred, must be clothed in mystery."

KR: Returning to the idea of the world that can be "read"—it seems that such an awareness would go hand-in-hand with an urgency to explore. What role has travel played in your life?

AE: I think you're right that the experience of reading or writing a poem and the actual experience of travel are very much the same for me, both of them arising out of that "urgency to explore" or "read" the world. The wonderful thing about travel is that all of your senses become aroused and engaged— it's kind of like the sacrament of communion or transubstantiation—so that transport and translation, both literally and figuratively, are manifest and inevitable. And whenever there is human experience, there is language, so whether it's foreign travel—with its necessity for literal translation—or travel to the backyard or across town or to a cookbook, the "transport" that may eventually inform a poem begins.

My poem "*Sans Serif*," from *Chez Nous* is one that I think of especially in this connection. There were two objects that gave rise to the poem: a piece of *opera* cake that I ate in Paris and a nineteenth-century green glass *flacon de l'opera* (a cylindrical glass flask which could be filled with brandy and, to keep it warm, tucked between the breasts by women attending the opera), which I found in an antique shop in Culpeper, Virginia. I myself became intoxicated with the sound of "op"—and the poem took off from there.

KR: French language and culture are a recurrent presence in your work. When did this passion arise?

AE: I'm not sure *when* my passion for all things French began, but it has been, as you say, of enormous importance for my work. It seems that at some point midway through my life (to paraphrase Dante), all of the things that most compelled me—language, architecture, food, wine, social ritual, the medieval world, art, music—especially Josephine Baker and Erik Satie—all of those things were French. And my love of American writers such as Hemingway and, especially, Gertrude Stein fueled my desire to discover what it was that could lead someone like Stein to become an expatriate and say, "America is my country and Paris is my hometown." In fact, the whole question of what and where a home can be—and the effects of having, naming, or not having one—very much informed the poems in *Chez Nous*. And, of course, there's just the French language itself—so gorgeous and sinuous, so evocative and endlessly intriguing.

In my second book, *Voice-Over*, as well as in my most recent book, *Tryst*, the language and culture of Italy, too, have been so much a part of my work. I've always loved what Stein says in her book *Paris France*: "After all everybody, that is, everybody who writes is interested in living inside themselves in order to tell what is inside themselves. That is why writers have to have two countries, the one where they belong and the one in which they live really. The second one is romantic, it is separate from themselves, it is not real but it is really there."

KR: ". . . a good translation / should have some memory / of its original language"—these lines in the final poem of *Tryst* could also speak toward the ekphrastic challenge of not only recapturing what has been portrayed but also in converting art into the language of poetry. . . .

AE: I love the connection you make here between ekphrastic poems and translation; both indeed do need to have some "memory" of their "original" language or medium and construction. I think that my process of writing about specific art works is the same as my process in writing any poem. Both begin with "divine details"—one notices, remembers *this* and *this* and *that*, then sees the *other*—and then those details make a shape that can eventually become a grid for a reader's/viewer's experience. But at the center of both is transport and transformation: things lift out of their original contexts in order to form a new and—as Jane Eyre says— "other and more vivid" experience.

KR: *Tryst* has turned toward more personal territory, mentioning family in several poems. There seems to be a little more of a narrative thread, too. Do you view these newer works as a departure or evolution in your writing?

AE: I'm not sure I know the answer to your question at this point, but at the moment I'm thinking that these newer territories are an evolution/extension of my previous poems. One of the reasons I say this is that both of the things you mention—the "more personal" and the inclusion of a little more narrative—just showed up in my work; it wasn't a conscious decision to include more of either. My poems have always felt—to me—already so intensely personal, although I can certainly understand their not coming across that way, in any conventional sense, to a reader.

But I think I've always been uneasy with "personal" detail and "narrative thread" in a poem, mostly because of their tendency to claim some "authentic" realm of experience that doesn't feel to me to be the experience the poem is really enacting or giving rise to. In any case, I'm intrigued by the way that a bit more of the personal and narrative have entered the poems—and my guess is that the narrative has trailed in behind the "personal" details and events. I don't think, however, that my newer poems have any more of an overall narrative structure, even though they contain narrative moments. I'm sure, too, that getting older necessarily creates more distance, an eerie simultaneous embracing of and estrangement from the personal details and events of early life, and that that distance enables all of those things to appear in different contexts. The writer Jeanette Winterson, in a recent essay, says something that seems to me to be related to the kind of "narrative" I'm most interested in; she writes, "Every work of art is an attempt to bring into being the object of loss."

KR: "Heart" melds the curious anecdote of the brain with a recollection. The tenacity of a seemingly precocious child, the parents waiting in the car—almost a reversal of what one might expect from family vacations—is delightful, but also tinged with a certain sadness. Is a mixing of tones and topics vital to your process?

AE: Yes, when I look at my work, it does seem that my poems are often structured by a mixing of tones and topics, although, again, my sense is that those mixtures and layers of things and experiences are already what constitute the world and our experience of it so that the job of the poem is to heighten our experience of our experience in some way. As Baudelaire says, "The only way to inhabit the present is to revisit it in a work of art." In "Heart," the scientific and anthropological details regarding the eating of dead relatives lead to the memory of the mother and the inevitable question posed by the poem of what her heart would taste like, which is another way of talking about the complexities and difficulties of intimacy with, and the ultimate loss of, the mother. So the image of the parents waiting in the car like "daguerreotypes"—fixed, immobile, and isolated from the speaker—works, I think, something like a metaphysical conceit, zooming back to the child's search for some ideal "antebellum" place and then to the image of Mary grieving for the dead Christ: the sense of loss and separation culminate and break through at that moment, that jarring turn in the poem, with the lines "this *what's the matter /* of the cerebellum."

KR: What do you look forward to in your next work?

AE: Well, I mostly look forward to just *having* new poems arrive, whatever they might be. Much of my new work, though, does seem to be very interested in Dante, especially his *Inferno, Purgatorio,* and *Paradiso.* Dante—in completely unpredictable ways—somehow got into the poems of my most recent book, *Tryst.* And now he's kind of taken over. What's compelling for me, continually, is the way in which the world of Dante and the contemporary world—Marlon Brando, even—speak to each other.

LANGDON HAMMER

The Voice Is Ready to Sing

A Review of Enchantée

"The poem must resist the intelligence,"Wallace Stevens wrote, but then he added: "almost successfully." Stevens isn't saying that poems must be unintelligible, but that a poem must not give in too quickly to our need to make sense of it. Rather, it must provoke, teasing the mind into action, into fresh experience.

Angie Estes—the author of four previous books of poetry, most recently, *Tryst*, a finalist for the 2010 Pulitzer Prize—would agree. Her poems revel in linguistic play, where the sound of words generates an associative logic that resists our intelligence, or at least our accustomed ways of making sense. Estes breaks language apart to see how it might be reconfigured. She pursues not sound over sense, but the sense sound itself makes, a tune that we can pick up—or better, that can pick us up and transport us—without our needing to know at all times what the words are saying.

"Nigh Clime" is about that musical transport. "Nigh," meaning what is near, comes from Old English. It suggests the diction of the King James Bible or Shakespeare and conveys a formal tone that coexists with intimacy. "Clime" is also archaic in feel, meaning a climate or surround, some specific environment. So the title points to a place that is nearby and familiar but also old, lit with "the glim / of ago."[1] Because we can hear "climb" in "clime," the place Estes invites us to is high. She calls it "the lingo / hill": a plane or latitude we climb to when we play with words just as kids do when toying with the building blocks of language, risking nonsense. But listen for the sense Estes is making. "The hem / of home," for instance, is not just a cleverly alliterative phrase, but also an image for the bedcover we put up under our chins at night. That "hem" makes the blanket seem like mother's (our mother tongue's?) skirt. There on top of the hill, which is also on top of the bed, poet and reader put their heads ("nogs") together. Now what is "nigh" is the leg of the reader or lover, secure beside the poet in the "niche" (so much softer than the nick) of time. This is a poem about the intimate, consoling, age-old pleasure of words on the tongue.

Not every Estes poem works in this intensely acoustic way. Images are the key in "Afternoon," which hints at a story: behind this poem's collage of memory and observation, linking birds' nests, push-up bras, and Elizabeth Taylor's sexy slip, is a daughter obliged to take on power of attorney for an aging mother losing her memory. And in "How to Know When the Dead Are Dead," Estes is a historical anthropologist meditating on the transition between life and death.

But "Recall" is a racing, intelligence-resistant, intelligence-transforming song. The sounds in that word, "recall," a noun and a verb, take Estes from the black mouth of a trout to shooting stars and the eyes of Sienese madonnas. She ends with a quotation from the phenomenologist Gaston Bachelard about how letters on the page become sounds in our mouths: *"we read ah / and the voice is ready to sing."*[2] This experience, commonplace and mysterious, is what Estes's poems offer us.

Notes

1. Angie Estes. *Enchantée* (Oberlin: Oberlin College Press, 2013), 15.
2. Ibid., 64.

JILL ALLYN ROSSER

Wonderlust
Angie Estes's Spiral Aesthetic

In Angie Estes's lexically charged realm, words and phrases are treated as delicacies in and of themselves, while in service to her poems' uniquely loopy, DNA-spiraling associative and logical trajectories. Her influences and muses are unabashedly eclectic, and their words, rhythms, perspectives, and images populate her oeuvre: references to Gertrude Stein, Marcel Proust, Emily Dickinson, Leonardo DaVinci, St. Augustine, Elvis Presley, Bernini, the sound of cows lowing, Percy Shelley, Maria Callas, Dante Alighieri, Rita Hayworth, Rachmaninoff, John Coltrane, Martin Heidegger, Henry James, and hosts of other fragments are shored in these richly textured poems. Certainly, many poets frequently allude to other writers and works of art, but I want to stress that Estes is not merely familiar with the works she plays off of; their presences are not the equivalent of touristic, drive-by sightings; rather, they strike the reader as objects of serious study taken to heart, authentically imbuing the thought processes dramatized in her poems. Estes has absorbed these influences the way a plant absorbs water and light: she gives herself over to flourishing her learning and aesthetic experiences and what she has made of them, in a kind of sacred homage—in rapture. Her fascination with the ricocheting movements of the mind, and their distortive resonance in the labyrinth of memory, is a driving force behind the linguistic somersaults, explosions, and palimpsests that color and animate her poetry.

In Estes's poems, language reassumes the authority that poets of earlier eras more readily accorded their words. Her speakers express themselves in a kind of meta-speech—while giving voice to an idea. Estes always has one ear trained on the words themselves, their sounds, associations, and etymologies, as they illuminate and often redirect her path through the labyrinth of thought, gauging their individual powers and histories. If we think of a poem as vehicle for vision's tenor, our current generation tends to view it as primarily a semantic/contextual journey rather than a sensual or aural one.

What I find particularly refreshing about Estes is the way she honors her instrument, the way a violinist buffs hers, rubbing rosin into the strings, and admiring the scroll and the shape creating the timbre; the way a jockey oils the saddle, strokes and brushes the horse, checks the fetlock, sniffs the oats before pouring them into the feedbag. In her poems, words represent at once the vehicle's wheels and its velocity, its actual physical manifestation and its potential for transport. My use of the word *transport* rather than *transportation* is a nod to Estes's meticulous and deeply double-entendred articulations: transport meaning at once physical movement from one place to another, and metaphysical transcendence.

In our contemporary culture, I think it's fair to say that a good number of our finest poets (and most of their readers), view words more purely as a means to communicate than as breathing, quasi-animate figures bearing—often concealing—fascinating etymological and connotational treasures that have their own communicative agendas. Here you might think I'm edging toward the suggestion that Estes's aesthetic has links to the concerns of language poetry, and there may be something in that, but not much. That is, the spirit of disjunction that presides over the poems of, say, Hejinian, Bernstein, and Watten, derives from a *mistrust* of language and its inevitable slippages, viewing it as a disappointing subversive power stealing authorial originality and control that must be manipulated *back*. However, Estes's leaps and swerves and weavings of disparate elements are more the product of an intense belief in language as a portal to some greater understanding of the world it purports to render. When Estes veers from bilingual puns and foreign idioms that seem uncannily to capture the slippery numinousness of our culture's mores into the charmed scrutiny of an ancient Italian fresco, careening from there into a contemplation of Nijinsky's biography, and then the description of a natural phenomenon, she is not demonstrating the speciousness of linear logic; rather, she revels in the linkages that are inherent in these partners in disparity. Estes unlocks that inherence; she celebrates the elasticity and polyvalent energy the mind generates and orchestrates in trying to embrace—or at least come to terms with—some essentially human meditation: loss, meaning/meaninglessness, beauty, mortality, truth, memory, desire. In many of her poems, this ricochet or spiral progression appears to be motivated by the fact that each new association allows the speaker to swerve away from a too-intense consideration of a painful truth best encountered at a slant.

An example of Estes's spiraling mind-motion mode is "*Verre Églomisé*" from her fourth book, *Tryst*. The reader is presented with fairly rapid-fire sequences of images and thoughts: we are ushered from the sight of a run-over squirrel being tugged by another squirrel off the asphalt, to a veteran's obverse-reverse tombstone inscriptions, to the practice of applying gold leaf for etching to the backside of mirrors, to an accidental excavation of a small statue of a fawn, to Ghiberti's *Gates of Paradise*, to the catacombs of Rome, and then back to Ghiberti. All of these contemplations culminate in the following observation about Ghiberti's narrative series of bronze relief panels: "the past / and future are flat; what's near is high // relief."[1] It then dives into a memory of her father's freckled arms resembling a fawn: "and beneath // his white hair ran a bristle // of rust, / which still grazes / my temples // though he's been // dead for years."[2] The poet then takes us back to squirrels with the fact that squirrel hair was used for the gilder's tip for handling gold leaf, which "sticks to the skin."[3]

Nestled slyly within this initially random-seeming assemblage of observations and memories is that wonderful statement about the past and the future, fusing the ekphrastic mode with the philosophical. We are led on this golden-mote-swirling journey to contemplate the tug-of-war between our compulsion to preserve an accurate account of what has happened to us and a wish to escape from unshakably haunting memories. This poem navigates between the desire to "mark" sites of loss (perhaps as a way of moving on from grief) and the wish to assist "the angels / in the resurrection."[4] Here Estes addresses a universal ambivalence: we are torn between the desire to open the gates of perception with "remarkable clarity" by viewing a design through glass, and conversely to draw a shadow over our sight. The reader is furthermore led by the juxtaposition of glass-viewing and angels to think of viewing this world "as through a glass darkly." Such reverse/obverse meanings vibrate throughout Estes's oeuvre, creating dynamic tensions in her writing that resonate and refuse to be resolved. Nevertheless, a new sequence of synapses has been discovered and unforgettably followed through. We feel a path has been distinctly blazed, an obliquely cogent thought-path that moves us closer to a truth or notion we can't fully absorb.

Another poem that amply showcases Estes's rich synthesis of verbal music and semantic wandering is "I Want to Talk About You," from *Enchantée*. The paradoxically fluid precision of images that carry us through the riffs of this poem is jazz-like in its circular returns to the primary thread of contemplation: the patterns of starlings shifting and morphing from design to design the way John Coltrane's "extended cadenzas" flirt with a melody but do not play it straight.

I see "I Want to Talk About You" as a kind of ars poetica: it so ably reflects the kind of fertile, morphing thought process that Estes validates again and again. This poem is lusciously aware of the words' sounds and lingers playfully over them, re-sorting, recombining, and recasting the syllables and letters they're made of: starlings tossing themselves wildly yet harmoniously like jazz notes about the sky flicker into "artlings," "last grins," and "art slings." They "roost rows to sorrows as they soar through aerial corridors and swerve / into the shape of a cowl that lengthens to a woolen scarf wrapping / and wrapping, // nothing at the center but throat. . . ."[5] The poem is a tribute not only to Coltrane but also possibly to some unnamed friend or lover, as the title suggests: the relationship is fluid, changing, surprising yet somehow always descanting on the familiar. These birds metamorphose into a visual massing of musical notes, adumbrating a kind of Cheshire-cat image of melody—nothing but throat—and pulling together like those "lips of the embouchure wrapping the saxophone's slurred // howl, scrawled signature of the sky."[6] This is masterful, ecstatic writing—it approaches Yeats's and Tennyson's ability to exploit a variety of vowels, linked by alliteration, in the service of exquisite music as both undercurrent to, and ultimately the manifestation of, her meaning. There are very few poets writing today who can come close to this kind of virtuosic phrasing and balance.

Another poem in *Enchantée* that veers wildly between divergent subjects is "Afternoon." Here Estes provides an extra hinge to keep the poem from flying apart. We begin with barn swallows' "mud cup" nests compared to push-up bras; then we move to the swallows themselves "slipping into [the nests] like boomerangs sliding back / to a hand." Mid-line, the speaker leaps from this hand into a memory of her mother teaching her to make a fist of her hand so as to slip it snag-free through nylon stockings. This spiral progression (in the space of six lines) leaves the reader curious to see how these images and memories can possibly dovetail, until it becomes clear that the poem is a meditation about one thing or state slipping into, or through, or out of, another. The clever device here is simply her regular repetition of the word *slip*, which recurs on average in every other line:

> . . . So let's slip into something more
> comfortable, like character or your native tongue,
>   and then later, after dinner, we can slip out
> early. But how far can the stargazer lilies walk
>   in their orange velvet slippers?[7]

This startling, gorgeously phrased question leads us to think about the speaker and her lover—are they stargazing, are they walking in a dream that can't last? The suggestion of sexual desire is unmistakable when we bump up against "Elizabeth Taylor in *Cat on a Hot Tin Roof,* leaning / against the door frame in her tight white / slip." In the following segment the word *slip* is omitted:

> . . . I knew it was time
> to take a break from writing poems
>   when the woman at the bank asked what kind of
> form I needed to have notarized, and I said *power*
>   *of eternity.*[8]

In the case of this charming anecdote the reader must supply the word herself: it's a slip of the tongue. One of the most apt and unforgettable images I have ever encountered about the slipperiness of perspective and consciousness is the one that ends this poem:

> . . . old films often flickered
>   and skipped, even occasionally slipped in
> a blank screen. It's how the world would look
>   through the eye of a lizard or bird: some nictitating
> membrane swept across like a curtain
>   at *The End* as we slip from consciousness into
> *oblivion* – an act of not exactly forgiveness
>   but an official forgetting that precedes
> what's then forgotten.[9]

The speaker and her friend have entered a theatre for a matinee, and are about to leave it. The experience of moving between two realms—the fictional and the real—is wonderfully evoked with that nictitating lid, which while it blurs or compromises direct perception also serves as protection for eyes that must transition frequently between water and air.

The suppression or distortion of memory can help to assuage a feeling of guilt, which is suddenly an issue. The question of forgiveness springs up here for the first time in the poem's final lines, and we might see this as merely another lexical palimpsest, given that one of the definitions of *oblivion* is "amnesty" or "pardon"; but I see it as the admission of a drama that has been lurking in the very skittishness of the lines. We sense the speaker is flitting from observation to observation partly to avoid some oppression that shadows her. Some fact has been omitted, avoided, flitted away from all poem long, and the speaker, emerging from the filmic fiction, is caught off guard and reveals this guilt, though not its cause. Art itself provides the pardon—the "official forgetting" clause of the blank screen, which is written into the art/reality contract; the blank screen acknowledges that we will have to forget this story in order to slip into the next, whether our own or another fiction; the only way to move through life without getting snagged is to "forget" our previous story or stage, where we've just been, to fist our hand and close it over what we are leaving behind.

It is interesting in light of the veiled personal drama in "Afternoon" to consider that Estes's second, third, and fourth books are more determinedly fact- and art-focused than *Enchantée*; her personal life was glimpsable only in the most oblique and privately coded references. This effectively self-stripped, observational mode, reminiscent of Marianne Moore's precise and quasi-omniscient voice, gave much of Estes's early work a Byzantine shimmer. But in *Enchantée*, Estes has allowed more of her personal life (or what sounds like authentic autobiographical detail) into her poems, and it adds an appealing dimension to her work. Whereas before the ekphrastic and classical references only grazed the quotidian and tended toward universal meditation, sometimes crowding out the particulars and their significance, here they can serve to limn and even magnify them. The arcane facts and art references in Estes's recent poems reinforce the tug of the personal, and evidence of a single life's particulars is now present in larger doses.

The presence of the autobiographical detail dominates Estes's "Note," despite the fact that the central subject is memory and its unreliability. This poem is launched by a communication the speaker receives about her mother:

> They wrote to say they'd found my mother *wondering*
> *in the garage*—like entering the ethereal sphere,
> I thought; *drawing near to its desire, so deeply*
> *is our intellect immersed that memory*

cannot follow after it, as if desire were a fugitive
dye made from the blue stars of the forget-me-
not and hell could be defined as that which cannot be
forgotten, the damned condemned to go on
like Paolo and Francesca in desire but unable to
recognize what could move them so. . . .[10]

This first stanza, referring to the mother's dementia, swiftly swoops
from the actual mother's experience to the line from Dante about
memory separating from desire when the latter is most intense
and "absorbing." It is the note's error of "wondering" in lieu of
"wandering" that creates the pretext for the narrator's own wan-
dering from the subject of her mother's memory loss. Not unlike
the skittish avoidance mode of the speaker of "Afternoon," the
note-writer's mistake has turned an object of serious concern into
something fascinating for this speaker to consider: perhaps, she
thinks, this is some form of "wondering" rapture, and the mother
has preempted the usual stages of her ageing and gone directly to
heaven: "like entering the ethereal sphere, I thought." This deflec-
tive thought process is common among children of ailing parents,
so this immediate movement away from the ostensible subject
feels utterly natural.

It is perhaps a welcome flight of fancy that leads the speaker
away from her anxiety and into the fictive sanctuary of Dante's
world, and beyond that into the art of painting, where certain colors
(blues in particular) are known to be fugitive, fading more quickly
than other pigments: "as if desire were a fugitive / dye made from
the blue stars of the forget-me- / not." From pigments in painting—
because she doesn't wish to return to the subject of the mother—
the speaker rides the current of her wandering into the botanical
sphere of forget-me-nots. The flower comes to mind because of its
fugitive blueness, but instantly the physical flower is superseded by
its name, which is suggestive of the tragedy of Paolo and Francesca,
whose desire has become a memory that haunts them without re-
vivifying the desire; there is horror in memory outliving a vestigial
feeling. In this situation one exists in constant yearning for the mo-
ments one can sort of remember, but too vaguely to reanimate
them. This feeble memory is in effect the hull and detritus of desire,
and yet evidence of the desire remains. Estes plants her line-break
between "forget-me" and "-not," which underscores the inescap-
able ghost of that desire. When we reach the end of the line with

"forget-me" and take a sigh of regret-tinged relief, we turn the corner and are met with the monosyllabically strong negation with a first-position caesura.

Each of the three succeeding stanzas of "Note" offers another example of incomplete loss or erasure. The second stanza relates to the speaker's mother obliquely:

> When I was a child, my mittens were attached
> to each other, their cord running under
> my coat from hand to hand like the blue
> veins in the clear plastic Invisible
> Man I assembled in the basement, and after
> he left assisted living, my friend's father
> kept asking, What if my mother dies
> again? What, I thought, if she slips off
> like a glove. . . .[11]

The mittens attach in memory automatically to the mother, who was probably the one who made sure those mittens were strung together. From there it is a small step into that childhood basement with the veined Invisible Man toy. The image of those veins combined with the mitten/mother attachment is reminiscent of the placental attachment of mother to child, and of course to the figurative attachment, which has existed since our earliest consciousness. Childhood memories of one's parent are at once among the strongest and the most compromised, since they are the oldest and have been "revised" far longer than any other.

In this same stanza, the friend's aged father's fear of losing his mother again demonstrates the incomplete erasure of the mother from his life; his desire for his mother's presence has separated from his memory of her death. When the speaker then wonders whether the mother might "[slip]off / like a glove," she may be wondering simultaneously how quickly or easily her mother's actual death could occur, and how ephemeral or recoverable her loss might afterward feel, given the persistence of her memory in its attachment to so many other formative memories.

The third stanza winds its way from this incomplete loss of the mittens/mother back to Dante, quoting his description of paradise as devoid of memory, leaving us with only a fugitively hued phantom memory, rather like a phantom limb:

In paradise,
Dante says, we will have only a memory
of having had a memory, now lost
like the photograph of my mother's great
grandfather printed from a negative made
from a photograph of a negative, which we
Xeroxed for keeps: it's the same old
story of the Perseids, their gray hair
streaking the sky the way ethereal
is streaked by real. . . .[12]

The subject of the mother is once more broached obliquely with the mention of increasingly faint reproductions of her maternal great-great-grandfather's photograph which, while the image has been repeatedly compromised, has nonetheless been "Xeroxed for keeps"—a possibly distorted memory vehicle, preserved the way the memory of a desire clings long past the presence or understanding of the desire. Another spiral is complete as once again the ethereal sphere is evoked by the Perseids: a cloud of debris ejected from a passing comet, existing past the active fact of the comet. The word *real*, Estes points out, is part of the word *ethereal*, and yet only one of these words signifies actual, present, apprehensible. The other is "streaked by," partakes of, the real.

In the final stanza, the poem spins through all the stages of its earlier orbit:

Like denizens
of the cadenza, cicadas scratching
their cicatrices, a star shines until day
begins to lighten the sky, the shining
gone though the star remains, not
shining but not yet gone, still
moving across the heavens right up
to the moment the sky turns
sky blue.[13]

Like cicadas that lie dormant for up to seventeen years, existing but not, the fugitive stars are "lost" with daylight but of course not lost, still faintly visible at dawn. When "the sky turns / sky blue," it has not changed, but a trick of light has altered our perception, just as our memory of an event can be altered by reconsideration or a subsequent event. If a particular shade of blue is characterized by being sky-like, and the sky turns black, then which is the ethereal, fugitive figment: sky or blue? If our memory is inevitably faded and compromised, then which is ethereal and which real: the objects of our memory or our memory itself? And if we are essentially the culmination of our memories, then when they fade we ourselves have entered an ethereal sphere like the mother in "Note" who was found "wondering in the garage."

Memory and its porousness or unreliability is a subject Angie Estes has dwelt on a good deal, notably in *Enchantée* in "Bon Voyage," "Sweet Gum," and "Revision." Proust and his struggle with pure memory are invoked more than once in Estes's poems, but it is in "Revision" that we are also reminded: "scientists maintain / that because a memory is altered each time / it's recalled, the original memory is the one // we can't know."[14] This may be so; but then we are recompensed with multifaceted gems created by our subconscious revisions, distracting ourselves from unpleasant facts, flinging them into artlings and different designs the way starlings swirl in the sky. These new memorial designs hold an array of delights and self-pardons that more than compensate for the loss of precision. The linguistic playfulness and logical wanderlust in Angie Estes's poems remind us that it is not the facts we love but their embellishments and associations; not the words we savor in these poems so much as the way their sounds and meanings forget themselves as they slip from one language or century or context to the next.

Works Cited

Estes, Angie. *Enchantée*. Oberlin: Oberlin College Press, 2013.
Estes, Angie. *Tryst*. Oberlin: Oberlin College Press, 2009.

Notes

1. Angie Estes. *Tryst* (Oberlin: Oberlin College Press, 2009), 67.
2. Ibid., 67.
3. Ibid., 67.
4. Ibid., 67.
5. Angie Estes. *Enchantée* (Oberlin: Oberlin College Press, 2013), 5.
6. Ibid., 5.
7. Ibid., 23.

8. Ibid., 23.
9. Ibid., 23–24.
10. Ibid., 26.
11. Ibid., 26.
12. Ibid., 26–27.
13. Ibid., 27.
14. Ibid., 58.

KEVIN CLARK

The Chapbook as Optic Lens

The distinctive pleasure in reading a chapbook of poems is usually twofold: first, the book is often a splendid physical artifact, a publication intended to please on a sensuous as well as literary level. Originally hawked on British street corners for a coin, the chapbook was normally quite short. Rarely more than thirty pages, the contemporary version is frequently printed on nicely textured paper. The cover art can be arresting, and, as in the case of Angie Estes's *Boarding Pass*, the text may be deeply impressed with hot type. Secondly, because most chapbook editors look for work that is more thematically focused than most full-length collections, a chapbook is almost never a miscellany of poems. The best volumes inevitably resonate with a kind of deep aural and contextual quality that comes from the poet's continuous study of a single subject as well as from the poet's personal voice.

In the case of the remarkable chapbook by Angie Estes, the virtually unbroken concentration on subject is so intense as to suggest that the poet employs poems as optic tools with which to see better her worlds, worlds in which meaning is beyond her everyday vision. Estes's book renders a state of compulsion and immersion, wherein the writer refuses to submit to the nearly prohibitive problem of seeing in an atmosphere ceaselessly refracted by myriad physical, metaphysical, and psychosocial issues, not the least of which is the writer's self-acknowledged limitations. Estes writes about the difficulties of attempting to establish identity in a world that conspires against meaning and freedom. Rather than surrender to chaos, the poet appears driven to isolate instances of clarity that help make sense of a swirling existence.

Estes's volume is unconventional in that individual poems have a broad, almost totemic feel to them, while the overall direction of the book seems to suggest a more specific theme. The book is especially intriguing in that individual poems are most often about the mysteries inherent in self-study, mysteries that arise from the inevitable subjectivity in the process, while the whole volume intimates a more definitively personal and political concern. Chapbooks encourage single themes, and this book emerges as a kind of archetypal inquiry into the problems of lesbian existence. Estes's verse is striking in its beautiful sexuality and complexity. Never politically or aesthetically simplified, the poems are at once finely crafted and imagistically ambitious. Charged in its chiseled diction, frank eroticism, and balanced resolutions, *Boarding Pass* shows readers willing to give it close attention not simply ideological points-of-view but—more importantly—the emotional fabric of lived life.

The prime difficulty for Angie Estes in *Boarding Pass* is making sense of reality in a culture unwilling to recognize—let alone accept—lesbian life. In a book already compressed by chapbook length, Estes's poems themselves are often marked by a kind of hard-wrought concision that serves to intensify an insistent desire to see the truth while simultaneously avoiding the illusions of a prettified world in which reality is camouflaged in cotton and lace. In all but two poems a dialectic is established in which the narrator addresses, often redresses, an unspecified "you." In the book's first poem, "The Iron's Credo," the "you" has asked the narrator why she goes "on this way, / travelling the same thin silver stream. . . ."[1] While the narrator admits she could have invited herself "to gaze at my own mirror," she rejects the solitary life of so many people isolated by their sexual preference and enters into a world of gay women's physicality and passion:

> But I chose instead to give pleasure to pleats
> and hung out with darts aimed at all manner of breasts
> because it is the journey I want:
> the slow, hot sashay
> down
> and back again.
> My profession—
> to dance with wrinkles
> to make water hiss.[2]

Though the poems are rich with encoded vaginal metaphors— "thin silver stream," "slivers," "pleats," "wrinkles"—and are concerned with the psychology of lesbian identity, the book is also about the need for clarity and resolution. In the title poem, for instance, which is positioned at the heart of the volume, the narrator's unique vantage as a person who happens to be lesbian is her "boarding pass" in this life. The quotidian problems of any life plus the special problems arising from this woman's myriad social pressures constitute the boarding pass that enables her to experience life from a distinctive perspective:

> Finally I tunnel out to the plane, tilt up
> into the night, and lean
> my head against that thin parenthesis
> while whatever's black outside
> leans back.
> And when the guard at the gate
> in Los Angeles asks
> do you have anything
> to declare, I answer no, nothing,
> nothing at all.[3]

Here Estes inverts the usual phallic symbolism of an airplane; the narrator finds haven inside the plane's hollow walls. And with the question of personal safety, of course, the issues of revelation and exposure arise. On one hand, the poem asserts that no one should have to reveal anything to anybody. On the other hand, Estes also seems to be asserting that her unique existence as a lesbian is also no reason she should have to be more revelatory than anyone else. She should have no more to declare to "the guard" than anyone else should.

Such surety of voice, however, does not characterize the entire book. Just as it is difficult for any one person to be consistently assured of their feelings, it may be specially demanding of a gay woman to remain steadily confident in understanding herself and her place in the world. One of the strengths of Estes's chapbook is its recognition of her own confusions. In what may be the volume's best piece, "A Poem Called Lost at Sea," the narrator imagines her artist's life as a boat that is, of course, lost at sea. While the danger of the circumstance is real, the narrator experiences some exhilaration as well, emerging perhaps from a new, unlikely freedom:

> All at once the sea would be personified
> And come to resemble every lover
> I ever knew. In the panic that followed,
> Line breaks of any kind would be forbidden;
> Everyone who threatened mutiny

Would be chained in the hold, and anyone caught
On deck without permission—my mother, for instance—
Could argue her view from the gangplank
While I lay on the tip of the bow, adjusting
The height of the horizon.[4]

The narrator is the captain, and what she writes is the law of her ship. If her mother or others have questioned the directions of her life, she can control their inquiries in the imaginative vessel of her poem. The poem is her power. What Estes discovers in the poem is that the confusion and unpredictability of her life are sources of ecstasy, and ecstasy linked to her sexual life:

One day, sun rotted, the sails
Would mercifully unzip, and naked lines of a poem
Called lost at sea could finally suggest
What happened: How your tongue stuck inside me like an oar,
How you and your boat kept turning, turning, turning.[5]

As in these lines, Estes's entire chapbook provides the reader with the emotional texture of a life under self-scrutiny. The resolve and commitment of the poet not only to continue to live a life unfairly marginalized but also to revel in the poetic examination of it is extraordinary and is somewhat reminiscent of Adrianne Rich's stance in her "Twenty-One Love Poems," originally published as a chapbook. Unlike Rich, however, whose sequence seems primarily motivated by the facts of injustice (as well as a failed lesbian relationship), Estes is more consistently erotic. The great energy of the book seems to be centered in the erotic, whether rendered indirectly or directly. "Poem in Winter," about remembering an old lover, ends with this striking declaration:

I remember only this:
the narcissus positioning themselves below.
Nothing else imagines the earth with slits
and then makes good on its promise.[6]

The comical "Visitations from the Muse," which is based on the notion that the poet enjoys a flirtatious relationship with a female muse, is Estes's candid explanation for the source of her work. The muse is seductive but plays hard to get, exposing her thighs, exposing the "blue tattoo" that reads "Desire."[7] Arriving home for dinner, the muse's breasts sway in time while her "slip flirts / in the fire."[8] In the last sequence of the poem, the narrator recalls that when the muse had first arrived, "the horse chestnut blossoms / sat up and took notice, pink and erect / in the skirted heaven."[9] The writer asks the muse to whisper whatever it is she has spoken to the flowers, "for the geraniums in all their vermillion / breathing, have never been / so loud."[10] The flowers, which are described in the spirit of Georgia O'Keefe's highly vaginal floral paintings, appear repeatedly through-out the volume as do so many other words that suggest sexuality: "river," "tongue," "lids," "lips," "slits," "slip," and so on.

Reviewing a book of poems about lesbian experience is tricky because one wants to take up the issue of a unique life formed *in part* by the special crosscurrents of lesbian existence, and yet one wants to avoid unintentionally limiting the scope of the poet's work to a political theme when, in fact, more than politics is at hand. Angie Estes's *Boarding Pass* is especially good not simply because of its imagery and diction but because of its breadth and depth.

Notes

1. Angie Estes. *Boarding Pass* (Atascadero, CA: Solo Press, 1990), 5.
2. Ibid., 5.
3. Ibid., 10.
4. Ibid., 17.
5. Ibid., 18.
6. Ibid., 9.
7. Ibid., 11.
8. Ibid., 12.
9. Ibid., 13.
10. Ibid., 13.

DOUG RUTLEDGE

Triste Trysts

In the title poem of her fourth book, Angie Estes notes that

> in *Vita Nuova*, Dante invokes
>   Beatrice to show how *tryst* was once
> the same word as *triste*, also related to
>   *truce*, how close it feels
> to *trust*.[1]

The poems that make up Estes's *Tryst* are often intimate meetings between the poet and the important people in her life, as well as between the poet and her audience. These meetings can be happy, but they are often very sad, as the poet seems to work on wordplay between the words *tryst* and *triste*. Moreover, these are often meetings that overcome the limitations of time and space. The poet accomplishes this by reintroducing us to lovers in literature, religion, art, music, and architecture across the span of human existence, so that these secret meetings of love become not simply intimate but also eternal.

   For example, in the opening poem, "You Were About," we meet a mysterious "you," with whom we assume the narrator has had an intimate meeting, a tryst, but we can only base that assumption on inferences that arise from the series of metaphors that punctuate the poem. The "you" of the poem exists in the mysterious reaches of the poet's memory and she was about to speak, but this aboutness is immediately compared to the *village perché* of Gorbio, a small French town in Provence. To *percher* in French is to hang out, so the village *perché* is perhaps the village n'er-do-well. The "you" is about to speak like the bum in a French village, a village built on a series of cliffs, so that the village itself seems about to fall into the ocean. Understand that it is the aboutness that is compared, directly to the bum and indirectly to the village, so that we have no idea where the "you" is; we only know that the fact that he or she was about to speak reminds the poet of someone who is always about to speak the way the houses of Gorbio are about to fall from a cliff.

The poet then begins a series of comparisons upon comparisons:

. . . You were
about face, about
time, streets cobbled
with diamonds like the bodies
of birds in Lalique's
ornament de corsage, Oiseaux
chanteurs. . . .[2]

Lalique was an art nouveau jeweler at the turn of the century, who specialized in diamonds. His work was on display at the Paris world's fair of 1900. So now the "you's" about face seems to be taking place in Gorbio or a similar village with cobblestone streets that shimmer like the diamonds in this art nouveau corsage, which also has singing birds. A corsage is of course a gift one gives a lover when one meets her, so the theme of intimate meeting continues to reappear. The birds in turn remind the poet of Beatrice, the idealistic love Dante once saw in church and who inspired and guided his spiritual odyssey through hell, purgatory, and heaven.

Now we must consider what the "you" was about to say in relationship to what Beatrice was about to say to Dante. Beatrice is most often about to chastise the poet. The moment Beatrice is waiting for the sun to rise is an interesting one in the *Divine Comedy*, because throughout the *Inferno* and most of *Purgatorio*, Beatrice is like a typical beloved of romance, in that she both challenges and guides him through spiritual trials that develop his character and encourage him to grow.

However, the sun in the *Divine Comedy* represents God and when it appears Beatrice will be eclipsed by a higher power, so this comparison might suggest that the poet is about to be left by the "you" or the "you" is about to be left by the poet or at least be overshadowed by something more important. It seems most likely that the poet would associate herself with Dante, which would suggest that the "you" inspired the spiritual growth of our poet. Perhaps she is about to leave her for something more important, and she was about to speak in order to prevent this separation. That would put the "you's" about face in an entirely new context, a context of rejection.

Perhaps that is why the poet continues not simply the religious theme but also the theme of penitence, for just as Dante is the quintessential penitent, going through hell and purgatory to make not simply himself but all of us ready for heaven, so each June penitents in Gorbio move in a procession up the winding streets of this medieval village at night with lamps made of the shells of snails, as the poet reminds us, to reach the church and its forgiveness.

This image of the lamps moving up the cobblestone streets reminds the poet once again of Dante, as he struggles up the mountain of *Purgatorio*. Dante must be forgiven for his pride, but perhaps the poet wishes to be forgiven for having rejected love. "According to Dante," the poet tells us,

> —everything ends
> with stars: like old sins
> or selves, their fleece is all of white
> we know, and they lead, then
> follow, everywhere we go.[3]

We are never really told about the tryst between the poet and the "you." Instead we learn of a French village with cliffs from which someone might fall; an art nouveau jeweler who made singing birds from diamonds, which were corsages and therefore symbols of love; and we learn of Beatrice leading Dante to a point at which Beatrice is eclipsed by something more important. And then we are reminded of forgiveness and that everything ends in stars. If the poet were leaving the "you," and being implored to stay by the "her," who was about to speak, that would explain why the poet continues to think about penitence. We can't really know what happened between the poet and the "you," but in asking us to think about it, the poet has asked us to consider a series of icons of human love and what they mean against a context of the human struggle for existence, separation, and forgiveness.

The theme of triste trysts is developed in two poems that consider family and World War II. "Gloss" begins with the poet as child being told that her Uncle Fred received a purple heart in the Second World War when the right side of his body was blown off. The child imagines "reddish blue figs / dropping from the hole / in his chest. . . ."[4]

Toward the end of the poem, as the poet refers to *Robert's Rules of Order*, she says that she wants to amend several things:

> . . . I move to amend
> the amendment and want
> to call the question, table
> the discussion, bed
> some roses, and roof the exclamation
> of the Great Blue heron sliding
> overhead, its feet following flight
> the way a period haunts
> a sentence:[5]

Part of the beauty of this passage stems from the fact that a Great Blue Heron looks like an exclamation point when standing still, and when it starts to fly one can easily imagine the feet being the period to a new sentence.

Now the child returns to her mother speaking of her brother, Uncle Fred. The image of a tryst exists here, if you think of love in the larger sense of including everyone one loves, because the poet, as a child, is meeting her uncle through the memory of her mother, yet it is a triste tryst, because of the uncle's horrible wounds. As the mother remembers her childhood and that of her brother, she also recalls plant life reminiscent of the child's image of "reddish blue figs / dropping from the hole / in his chest . . . :"

> . . . she said that
> on the mountain where they grew
> up, there were two kinds
> of cherries—red heart
> and black heart—both of them
> sweet.[6]

Clearly, the red and black hearts of the cherries recall both the purple heart of the uncle's wound and the reddish blue figs the child imagined filling the holes in her uncle's chest. Both are images of the child hurting for the loss of an uncle, whom she can only meet through her mother's memory, but they are also images of the child healing through her own imagination and through the love she can sense in her mother's voice.

"Nevers" is another poem concerned with World War II that is full of triste trysts. It opens upon an evening when the poet and perhaps a friend are attending a performance of Pucini's *Madama Butterfly*. In the opera, Cio-Cio San, Butterfly commits honor suicide, caused by a triste between cultures, reminiscent of military occupation. War will soon come up in this poem, but not before we are asked to consider another opera, *Manon,* by Massenet. *Manon* is an opera of triste trysts. Manon, a sixteen-year-old girl on her way to a convent, meets and runs away with Des Grieux. He asks his father for permission to marry Manon, but dad has his son arrested, and Manon is seduced by the wealthy Brétigny. Now Manon bemoans the loss of their table, "*notre petit table,*" which Estes mentions in the poem. This is the table at which she and Grieux have met and had their daily trysts, but which she now must leave. The plot quickly reverses itself, as Manon becomes the mistress of a wealthy man and Des Grieux becomes an Abbé at the seminary of St. Surplice. Soon Manon and Des Grieux meet and decide to run away together once again. However, Manon's desire for wealth gets them in trouble during a gambling match. Manon is arrested and about to be sent to the colonies. In the process, she becomes ill. During their final tryst, Manon dies in Des Grieux's arms. Manon sacrifices love and life for wealth, whereas Pinkerton refuses to take Butterfly's love seriously. Both moves violate the sanctity of tryst and seem in some ways to make possible the horrors that the poet moves on to recollect.

The poet continues to develop images of meetings, but now we have shifted back to Japan. When one meets new neighbors in Japan, one gives them noodles, the name of which means "we moved near you." However, the theme of meetings quickly becomes darker, as the focus shifts to a clash between the honor culture of Madam Butterfly and the more happy-go-lucky, technological culture of America. The honor culture could not let itself be conquered in the mid-1940s, so the technological culture attacked it with a bomb. This was not simply a tryst, but was also a triste.

> above Hiroshima, the cloud
>   was not a room for two
> but a parachute, a pair of
>   shoes reaching for ground that continues
> to deflate.[7]

The cloud resulting from the nuclear blast is not a meeting place, a room for two, but a parachute. Indeed, it has the look of a parachute, but of course a parachute is designed to save a life, while the whole point of the nuclear explosion was to take as many lives as possible. The explosion of the atom bomb reminds the poet of the film

Hiroshima Mon Amour. The plot of this film revolves around a series of trysts between a French nurse and a Japanese soldier who meet shortly after the war. The nurse simply adopts the French word for she, "*elle*," and the soldier adopts the word for he, "*lui*." In that regard they become the quintessential man and woman meeting, but they must meet against a backdrop of war, which destroyed tens of thousands of people all at once, and then thousands more gradually. The bomb represents the inability of two cultures to meet, while the quintessential love affair argues profoundly that any two people can realize the opportunity to understand and even love each other in spite of cultural conflict.

The name of the French town, *Nevers*, that gives the poem its title offers a pessimistic tint to this poem about meeting, but this idea that when two people meet on their own they can overcome the differences of culture, and even the differences of time and space, offers the poem its optimism, or as "You Were About" suggested, the feeling that "everything ends in stars." Indeed this optimism not only makes the uplifting conclusion of the poem possible but also makes possible the poet herself:

> Now the moon
> is a missing plate, facing
> each evening as if it were the telegram
> my father sent my mother
> in 1944 on the day before
> they married saying *Arriving*
> *tomorrow. Stop. Don't stop.*[8]

And so the war ends, which is a triste meeting between cultures, and love begins, which is a tryst or a secret meeting between people who care about one another. Similarly, the poem begins with an honor suicide of a Japanese woman, when her American military lover abandons her, and it ends when an American soldier leaves the Japanese war and returns to marry his prewar sweetheart. Sad meetings and the fulfilling ones, *Tryst* is filled with each sort, and as the reader struggles to understand their significance, he or she comes to understand the beauty, the history, and the meanings of meetings in the cultural tradition of the West.

Notes

1. Angie Estes. *Tryst* (Oberlin: Oberlin College Press, 2009), 64.
2. Ibid., 1.
3. Ibid., 2.
4. Ibid., 25.
5. Ibid., 25–26.
6. Ibid., 26.
7. Ibid., 57–58.
8. Ibid., 58.

MARK IRWIN

"Ethereal Streaked by the Real"
Desire, Language, and Memory in Three Poems
by Angie Estes

In Angie Estes's "Note," a wonderfully unassuming title of a com-
plex and layered poem, the speaker proposes four personal stories in
counterpoint along with two abstract notions of desire and mem-
ory from Dante's *Divine Comedy*. Estes's four skeletal stories include
"mother *wondering in the garage"*; childhood mittens attached with a
cord; an amnesiac father asking, "What if my mother dies / again?";
and a photograph of a photograph of a great-grandfather. What's
fascinating is the facility with which Estes juxtaposes real, tangible
events with metaphysical concepts in a manner that recalls Dickin-
son's phrase "And then a Plank in Reason, broke."[1] Here's "Note"
in its entirety:

> They wrote to say they'd found my mother *wondering*
> *in the garage*—like entering the ethereal sphere,
> I thought: *drawing near to its desire, so deeply*
> *is our intellect immersed that memory*
> *cannot follow after it,* as if desire were a fugitive
> dye made from the blue stars of the forget-me-
> not and hell could be defined as that which cannot be
> forgotten, the damned condemned to go on
> like Paolo and Francesca in desire but unable to
> recognize what could move them so
>
> ★ ★ ★
>
> When I was a child, my mittens were attached
> to each other, their cord running under
> my coat from hand to hand like the blue
> veins in the clear plastic Invisible
> Man I assembled in the basement, and after
> he left assisted living, my friend's father
> kept asking, What if my mother dies

again? What, I thought, if she slips off
like a glove

★ ★ ★

          In paradise,
Dante says, we will have only a memory
of having a memory, now lost
like the photograph of my mother's great
grandfather printed from a negative made
from a photograph of a negative, which we
Xeroxed for keeps: it's the same old
story of the Perseids, their gray hair
streaking the sky the way ethereal
is streaked by real

★ ★ ★

Like denizens
of the cadenza, cicadas scratching
their cicatrices, a star shines until day
begins to lighten the sky, the shining
gone though the star remains, not
shining but not yet gone, still
moving across the heavens right up
to the moment the sky turns
sky blue.[2]

The poem opens with the play on words "my mother *wondering*
/ *in the garage*," which hints at a form of dementia in old age that the
poet compares with "entering the ethereal sphere" of Paradise,
which in turn conjures the memorable opening quote from Dante's
Paradiso: "*drawing near to its desire, so deeply / is our intellect immersed
that memory / cannot follow after it.*"[3] Estes finds the poem's entire
architecture here (and this is a poem of wonder and marveling as it
wanders) and rightfully so, for it is our intellect along with memory
that deteriorates with age, while desires continue, lived perhaps
more purely through memory. Ideally the souls in Dante's *Paradiso*
swarm toward lights of the Empyrean with such fervor that human
intellect and passion merge with divine intellect and love, an alle-
gory that mirrors and heightens Dante's earlier guides, Virgil and
Beatrice (divine reason and love). Continuing to guide Dante in
Paradiso, Beatrice's beauty is so intense that it won't remain in

Dante's memory long enough to be recorded. In *Canto XXX*, Dante watches the constellations fade at dawn, and in doing so makes a comparison to the Primum Mobile's point of light disappearing as he and Beatrice advance toward the heavens. Estes likens such pure desire to a "fugitive dye made from the blue stars of the forget-me-not" (a strong metaphor since all the images in Estes's poem are forgotten or lost). Paradoxically, *what can't be forgotten* for Paolo and Francesca (trapped in their illicit desire) becomes hell and continues to move them in a negative way.

Estes—in a deeply human gesture—creates a kind of paradise for all of the aged beings in the poem as their gray hair streaks our perceptions the way the Perseids' "gray hair" streaks the sky, "the way the ethereal / is streaked by the real"—a memorable image: our heightened mortal moments streaking a bit of light onto the heavens the way the northern lights might, or a child's random drawing on an Etch-a-Sketch is remembered.

Recalling childhood, the speaker finds the cord attaching her mittens "like the blue / veins in the clear plastic Invisible / Man I assembled in the basement. . . ." These are ultra-tangible moments luridly connected to memory: a child's forgetfulness and the Invisible Man's graphic, detailed, yet troubling immodesty! Estes uses these two images as prelude to a startling transition:

> and after
> he left assisted living, my friend's father
> kept asking, What if my mother dies
> again? What, I thought, if she slips off
> like a glove[4]

A memorable simile to say the least: a repeated death like a mitten lost again and again. Can you follow Estes's invisible "cord?" It's part of her high art, or as Pierre Boulez said of Stravinsky's *The Rite of Spring*, "The art of composition is the art of transition."[5] Estes here continually attempts to transition us to the divine through images that braid and transcend time.

The divine waxes as memory wanes in stanza three as the speaker reminds us "In paradise, / Dante says, we will have only a memory / of having had a memory," since our desire will join the Divine Intellect and memory will fade. Estes wonderfully complicates this with the photograph of a photograph of a great-grandfather made from a negative, then Xeroxed. It's the Xerox the family keeps; its blurred reality attempting to streak the ethereal. One recalls Gerhard Richter's *Liebespaar im Wald* (Lovers in the Woods),[6] a painting projected onto canvas from the photograph of two lovers in a forest, after the photo had been Xeroxed multiple times in order to muddy it. Finally, the couple's reaching arms and torsos blur, along with their desire, toward the trunks and limbs of the trees.

"Note" ends with a keen synesthesia of the aural, tactile, and visual: "cicadas chirping, scratching their cicatrices" (the French for scars), and a star fading in morning light. Yet once again it's the heightened language here, the hyperreal words streaking the ethereal. Estes tells us: "Like denizens" (things adapted to a new place) "of the cadenza" (a flourish at aria's end) "cicadas chirping, scratching their cicatrices . . ." The poet inflects the onomatopoeia of two Latinate words: cicatrice and cicada.

And "Like denizens / of the cadenza, cicadas scratching / their cicatrices, a star shines until day / begins to lighten the sky . . . ," Estes's simile leads us like the major clef introducing a bar of music: here where a star performs an aria of silence, "right up / to the moment the sky turns / sky blue." Through continuing metaphor, Estes also leads us back to Dante's complex notion of desire and memory.

An interesting and final note here is that only the last of the poem's four sections ends with punctuation—here a period. This lack of end-section punctuation reinforces the poem's notion of desire in the first part ("a fugitive / dye"); the amnesia in the second part ("slips off / like a glove"); and the fading of memory in the third part ("ethereal / streaked by real"). All this allows the work to become one fabric of desire, language, and memory as the poem's asterisks between sections meld with the fleeting Perseids.

Although Estes's "I Want to Talk About You" does not employ the contrapuntal narrative pattern of "Note," it further orchestrates notions of desire, language, and memory. Here the narrative triangulation operates around the description of starling flocks near Oxford, England, a John Coltrane piece, along with a reference to Dante's *Inferno*, all wrapped into a love poem for the poet's partner. Just as love renews one's vision of the world, so Estes's poem renews language and our relationship to it.

The renowned French poet Yves Bonnefoy believed that "Poetry is an act by which the relation of words to reality is renewed."[7] Estes accomplishes this act in her love poem, written in twelve couplets, while marveling at flocks of starlings as she recreates and improvises our relation to the world via these birds. Here's the richly alliterative opening:

> when starlings swell over Otmoor, east of Oxford, as the afternoon
> light starts to fade. Fifty flocks of fifteen to twenty starlings, riff raff
>
> who have spent the day foraging in fields and gardens suddenly
>   rise
> like a blanket tossed into the sky, a reveling that molts sorrows to
>   roost
>
> rows, roost rows to sorrows as they soar through aerial corridors
>   and swerve
> into the shape of a cowl that lengthens to a woolen scarf wrapping
>
> and wrapping, nothing at center but throat: thousands of single
>   black notes
> surge into a memory called *melody*, the lovers damned but driven
>   on[8]

Remarkably, through the richness of language, assonance, and alliteration, the birds fashion a cowl that "lengthens to a woolen scarf wrapping // and wrapping, nothing at the center but throat": a tactile image of love rising from the aural in which the center becomes all throat, all singing. Estes's command of language, in which words regenerate new words ("sorrows to roost / rows"), reminds one of Plath's work. Here the pianissimo will darken ("shape of a cowl") as this poem veers toward those despairs that lovers encounter "damned but driven on / by violent winds," alluding to Dante's *Inferno*.

Here again Estes will also renew memory via image and language as "thousands of single black notes / surge into a memory called *melody*," that architectural spine of music. The poet continues pushing the image until the starling wings bear the damned lovers

> *along in broad and crowded ranks*, extended cadenzas to pieces that
>
> never get played, brochure for the flared tip that begins with the
>   tongue
> and lips of the embouchure wrapping the saxophone's slurred
>
> howl, scrawled signature in the sky. Thousands fly but never collide[9]

Through a kind of *jazz-riffing* of her own, Estes will renew love's violent memory through language. These wings bearing lovers become "extended cadenzas" or flourishes, a "brochure" or prospectus for the "flared tip that begins with the tongue / and lips of the embouchure wrapping the saxophone's slurred // howl, scrawled signature in the sky." The word "brochure" is swallowed in "embouchure" (mouthpiece) as the sax provides the aural equivalent of these starlings swerving across sky.

What's most enthralling about this poem, whose title refers to John Coltrane's performance of that Billy Eckstine song, is Estes's own improvisation as she creates anagrams of words (*art slings / grass lint, / snarl gist, / gnarls sit*) and induces an avian reality as the poem ends:

like the wave's rain of sand or words falling

out of a sentence: *art slings*, we call them, *grass lint, snarl gist, gnarls sit*. Art slings them this way, *last grins*, art slings swell, rove

over, red rover, red rover, send *artlings* right over, *artlings rove, moor to swell,* write Otmoor all over[10]

Again the speaker becomes her subject matter—starlings, matters of the heart—and embodies the place "Otmoor, east of Oxford," until "the relation of words to reality is renewed" and origin of place is recreated: red rover, red rover, send *artlings* right over, *artlings / rove, moor to swell,* write Otmoor all over." A common child's play-song summons the heavens, birds, and writes "Otmoor all over" as Eros not only reaccomplishes place but recreates it.

In Estes's "Wont to Do," she also juxtaposes real events in contra-puntal narrative with metaphysical concepts of memory, time, and desire that she transforms through language. Here, four consecutive narratives in the first four stanzas (night to morning, description of a Matisse painting, description of an elderly aunt speaking, and the return to night/night blooming cereus) are contrasted with three final images in the last three stanzas: *ductus*, April/chartreuse, hope-lessness/*Inferno*. Estes orchestrates notions of time, memory, and de-sire through the architecture of her title and the word "wont," which suggests "accustomed" or "habitual," another dangerous form of memory since there are good and bad habits. It was the poet John Wheelwright who said, "All habit is evil,—even speech;

/ promises prefigure their own breach."[11] Estes opens her poem with the personification of earth rotating toward morning and the salient cry of a cardinal: *cheek cheek cheek.*

> As it turns morning into light, you can hear
> the earth creak on its axis, release the red *cheek*
> *cheek cheek* of a cardinal.[12]

As the "earth creaks on its axis," the word creak releases the ono-matopoetic "*cheek.*" Again, the synesthesia is powerful as we imagine the cardinal's red coat through flush rhyme. The first stanza also sets up the notion of cyclical time/habit that will end in stanza four with evening.

Stanza two, ekphrastic in nature, describes Matisse's *Luxe, Calme et Volupté* (a title taken from Baudelaire's "L'invitation au Voyage") as the speaker types/"clicks" the title's words out on the keyboard:

> "the ticking   of a clock, while   the naked bathers
> go on like   melody beneath the sun's   cymbal . . ."

Here vulgar time (click/tick) is juxtaposed with a higher cyclical time where the sun is embellished with sound's "cymbal." The poet employs emphatic spaces throughout this stanza that mimic the act of painting: the tactile. Estes describes the way Matisse finds the visual equivalent of *desire recalled through memory* through the painting's center:

> The center of   the painting   is silent: a small boat
> with its sail   X   beached   on the red bank
> of pleasure—its hyphenated   shore—the way   the memory of
> pleasure   moors in the brain—violet,   yellow, orange, green
>   bricks
> mortared   with the white   of day.[13]

Stunning here the way "the red bank / of pleasure" turns violet in memory. Red combined with blue (over time) creates violet. Estes allows us to feel time form through color.

Stanza three, one of the most memorable, spills into the separated stanza four as the poet recalls a memory of her elderly aunt speaking, which recalls switchbacks in a Cézanne *nonfinito* painting that will in turn morph into a pun with the plant known as the night blooming cereus: "When night blooms, / it's serious: the poplar spills / soprano and warns the grackles / of my heart." Again, the visual morphs into the aural as a poplar spills birdsong into the less comfortable (grackles) emotions of the heart. Here is the prior stanza leading into the fourth as it creates a geographic-intaglio image from an aunt's troubled speech.

> When she turned 87, my aunt spoke in sentences, long
> and chiseled like the paths worn by the hooves
> of cows on the hillside, switchbacks
> winding up toward a peak as in Cézanne's
> *nonfinito* paintings, where you can see

> what isn't there.[14]

Sentences like "chiseled paths" from cow hooves provide a painful demarcation of time as they climb like the switchbacks in a Cézanne painting. As Cézanne grew older, he left more and more bare, unfinished spaces on his canvases. The unpainted canvas bothered many critics, but for the painter it was a way to integrate absence, complement his broken lines, and allow the viewer to participate. Here Estes also seems to be mimicking the souls in Dante's *Divine Commedia* as they move upward from purgatory to paradise.

Stanza five creates architecture/geography through etymology in an innovative and memorable way with the definition of *ductus*.

> In medieval rhetoric, the path or way through
> a text is called *ductus,* as in duct
> and aqueduct: John of Patmos
> must finally eat
> the book.[15]

Writing creates a stream that we must navigate. John of Patmos must devour all the parts of his *Revelations*. Here the *ductus*, or path through the text, refers to Revelations 10:10: "And I took the little book out of the angel's hand, and ate it up; and it was in my mouth sweet as honey: and as soon as I had eaten it, my belly was bitter."

Estes's last two stanzas find the emotional equivalent of color through desire and common memory as the author considers again the plight of souls in *The Inferno*.

Fill like April with chartreuse, swell
against the sky's gunmetal blue.

———————————

It's where we dwell, Dante says:
cut off from hope, we go on
in desire, always close
to won't.[16]

To "Fill like April with chartreuse" recalls the liqueur suffusing
within a glass as it swells against the Dantean "gunmetal" sky. By
this point in the essay you probably recognize that Estes is also a
sophisticated visual artist: a painter (with words) of the first class.
She ends her poem with a moral lesson that the reader must deci-
pher through language in a kind of Nabokovian wordplay. Just as
the souls in *Inferno* must compensate for lack of hope through de-
sire, the author reminds us that if we choose this path then "wont"
or habit can morph to "won't" and our moral lives will sketch their
grief, their past and selfish *want* against a gunmetal sky.

Works Cited

Bonnefoy, Yves. *Times Literary Supplement.* August 12, 2005.
Boulez, Pierre. "Lecture: Master's Concert." The Cleveland Institute of
Music, October 1983.
Dante. *Paradiso,* trans. Robert and Jean Hollander. New York: Random
House, 2007.
Dickinson, Emily. *Complete Poems of Emily Dickinson,* ed. Thomas Johnson.
Boston: Little, Brown, 1960.
Estes, Angie. *Enchantée.* Oberlin: Oberlin College Press, 2013.
Wheelwright, John. *Collected Poems.* New York: New Directions, 1983.

Notes

1. Emily Dickinson. *Complete Poems of Emily Dickinson,* ed. Thomas John-
son (Boston: Little, Brown, 1960), 129.
2. Angie Estes. *Enchantée* (Oberlin: Oberlin College Press, 2013), 26–27.
3. Dante. *Paradiso,* trans. Robert and Jean Hollander (New York: Random
House, 2007), 53.
4. Estes, *Enchantée,* 26.

5. Pierre Boulez. "Lecture: Master's Concert." The Cleveland Institute of Music, October 1983.

6. Gerhard Richter. *Liebespaar im Wald* (170 cm x 200 cm). The Israel Museum, Jerusalem, Israel, 1966.

7. Yves Bonnefoy. *Times Literary Supplement*, August 12, 2005, 2.

8. Estes, *Enchantée*, 5.

9. Ibid., 5.

10. Ibid., 6.

11. John Wheelwright. *Collected Poems* (New York: New Directions, 1983), 94.

12. Estes, *Enchantée*, 32.

13. Ibid., 32.

14. Ibid., 33.

15. Ibid., 33.

16. Estes, *Enchantée*, 33.

B. K. FISCHER

"Words remain *en pointe*"
Angie Estes's Choreographic Poetics

The word "choreograph" yokes writing to harmonized movement. The Greek *khoreia* for chorus, coupled with *graph* for writing, yields the term for the work of composing patterns and movements for dancers, and for the theory and annotation of that art. Drawing on dance lexicon and chorus-writing of several kinds, Angie Estes's "Cache," from her book, *Enchantée*, presents clauses in a composition that both indicates and emulates choreography:

> We filled the room
> with stargazer lilies, the scent
> of a sentence when it's ready
>
> to speak. Relevant: the nuns folding
> from *relevé* to *grand plié*
> as they touch the stones
>
> in Saint Gervais then kiss
> the tips of their fingers. . . .[1]

The first-person plural positions the speaker within a chorus that "filled the room," but the next prepositional phrase replaces the suggestion of a group, over the space of the line-break, with lilies, and then with a sensory permutation—a scent—that gives way to Estes's own primary medium: the sentence. Against this theatrical backdrop, watching a performance and punning on the relevance of a gesture of uplift (*relevé*) and descent (*grand plié*), Estes's sentence moves from "Île" to an "account of *I'll*," from an island in the "orchid lei" of the Seine to the Carmelite nuns in Saint Gervais in the Marais, then to the actualization of the poet's language itself:

> [. . .] You taught me
> tart grammar, how to keep
> thin slices of apple on edge

in *crème pâtissière* the way words
remain *en pointe* in a poem.[2]

With characteristic synaesthetic layering, Estes introduces a gustatory image, the tart apple in the pastry, then enfolds a dance term within a figure for poetry. "Cache" leads the reader clause by clause to the "grammar"—the structures, mechanisms, and movements—that makes it possible for her to hold up and make "relevant" a word or phrase. A cache is a hoard, a collection of artifacts, as well as short-term memory made available for quick retrieval, and it serves as an emblem for Estes's poetics, where copious materials, ever-changing scenes and details, move and shift across the surface of poems, readily at hand for contemplation, comparison, and wit. In the process, as references move on and off stage, sometimes a word is raised "*en pointe*" and "on point"—apt and affecting, poignant and piercing.

Tracing references to dance across Estes's five books reveals not only a recurrent theme, a rich lode of imagery and anecdote, but also the arc of an evolving poetics where perceptual and sensual details unfold in spaces that suggest keenly orchestrated temporality and embodied movement. Dance is for Estes not only a topos, a stopping place for appreciation, but a mechanism and a recurrent metaphorical vehicle. A "dance move" in her poems is a piece of hardware, a hinge or screw or pulley, in the "small or large machine" that each of her poems is:

> Now geese hurry across
> the sky like ballerinas, wings
> flung back: *plissé,*
> *plié.* If it were
> travesty, a change of
> dress, I'd call out *belong,*
> *dearest, lengthening of day,*
> *May until summer: tarry,*
> *linger, don't be*
> *long: long reign, long*
> *live.*[3]

A dance metaphor, hinged on terms for "puckered" and "bent," invites the reader into a subjunctive space—"if it were"—where the pretense of metaphor as costume change, a substitution of "vest"-ment, becomes a series of directions for the beloved to linger and return.

An Estes poem, like a choreographic composition, is predicated on a map of movements that reveal "invisible structures." The epigraph to *Enchantée*, from the legend of an excavation map below a Roman church, indicates three ways to read the features of a layered space. The middle category in the key suggests the formal zone where both dance and her poetry reside: "structures not visible but about whose position we are certain."[4] This category differs, on one hand, from "structures that are visible," the static structures of architecture and the visual arts that remain in space, and also differs, on the other hand, from "structures thought to have existed," those that are speculative, purely linguistic. An Estes poem, like a dance, exists in the middle condition, perceivable but in flux. As Wendy Lesser observes, dance, like poetry, is a temporal art—it unfolds through time, it *elapses*.[5] Like dance, a poem can be repeated, but it must proceed in time, cannot be apprehended (or perceived) all at once. Moments in Estes's poetry that make reference to dance expose the "invisible structures" that inform her temporal epistemology—a mode of knowledge and revelation that unfolds through moving moments that do not hold still.

Estes's frequent references to the visual arts and art history have received abundant critical notice, but her choreographic forays and analogies, enmeshed and braided into other strands of reference, have been noticed less often. The examples that follow reveal the extent to which dance is a structural analogy in Estes's work, a set of principles on which she draws to orchestrate the expansive gestures and sensory surges her poems comprise. Basic choreographic principles can be usefully applied to the phrasing and pacing of her poetic forms: gesture, locomotion, elevation, falling, turning, stillness. Moreover, Estes's poetic technique reveals an affinity with the kinds of coordination called for in dance composition, such as the controlled transference of weight, with one idea or image transitioning rapidly to the next, shifting the center of gravity mid-motion. From her first collection to her latest, Estes is as "dancerly" as she is painterly, to use Sandra Lim's term—dance invites another kind of ekphrastic impulse, one that is fundamental to an obsession with syntax. A poem's syntax and lineation—the invisible structures of the sentence intersecting the visible structures of the line— suggest choreographic space, and they also invite the paradoxical possibilities of imagining the body's syntax. Estes is keenly aware of the proprioceptive sense—the body's self-conscious awareness of its extension in space, and its intuitive understanding of how its movements coordinate with its objecthood. The poem-as-dance becomes an expression of yearning to connect by extension or translation, to re-hinge subject and object, position and place, and then to land, transitively, in a condition of linguistic embodiment.

Although classical ballet and its formal spaces figure prominently among Estes's dance references, she also draws on folk dance to dramatize moments of domestic give-and-take. Dedicated to her mother, "The Dance of the Sheets," from her first book, *The Uses of Passion* (1995), invokes dance in a scene of origins and maternal transmission of knowledge:

> After do-si-doing all those years
> the steps are learned at last
> steps we practiced over and over
> out back
> under the clothesline
> you in white boots
> indivisible from the glittering snow
> as you whipped away
> yet another bleached sheet
> to hang in front of my frozen eyes.[6]

Practicing steps "over and over" in the space of similarly repetitive domestic labor leads to a moment of attunement "at last," and square dancing becomes a figure for difficult harmony. "Do-si-doing" invokes the "doing" of chores—hanging clothes in winter, even in the aesthetic "glittering" that unites boots and snow, is not easy work—and the bleached sheet on the clothesline becomes a stage curtain, a scrim for a long-sought moment of concord:

> On this at least we finally agree—
> that it's left over right
> shake and turn
> fold in the middle.
> And as I approach you now
> corner to corner
> eye to eye
> I lower myself to
> myself
> on this white gleaming mirror
> arms outstretched, a blinded lover
> amazed

that we dance
together.[7]

The clause "On this at least finally we agree," with its inverted syntax, betrays some exhaustion. The act of folding sheets becomes a difficult dance, the symmetry of "corner to corner" preparing for the falling action of the line-break from "I lower myself to" to "myself." Self-recognition occurs in a set of physical gestures that requires two bodies to coordinate with each other: "left over right / shake and turn / fold in the middle." Energizing the well-practiced duet is the amazement of embrace.

Estes finds choreography in laundry, and also, from the outset of her career, in a variety of other physical disciplines. *Voice-Over* (2002), the collection that launched her to national prominence with the 2001 FIELD Prize and the Alice Fay di Castagnola Award from the Poetry Society of America, dwells frequently in the proprioceptive sense. Forceful enjambment—the whiplash of a line-break between subject and verb, the onrush of a break on a present participle—underscores the tensely controlled vector of a horse race:

[. . .] Suspended in some region
between heaven and earth, horse and jockey
lean into homestretch, twin arcs flying
above the track: with only one hoof touching dirt, they
tilt toward some finish they can only imagine.[8]

Elsewhere, an opera singer's exertions are portrayed as equally physical, envisioned in space that has the solidity of carpentry, until that figure in turn morphs into fabric, and then into spirit: "Mortise and tenon, tongue and / groove, tongue-in-cheek, the tenor / holds the note until it dovetails / in air like the white kerchief of / the Holy Spirit" in Massaccio.[9] Moving as they often do from one realm of making to another, Estes's lines "dovetail / in air," an intangible path of motion and mind-space that is nonetheless palpable. She questions her own practice and answers with another instance of choreographic prowess:

[. . .] And where is syntax,
sentence, *my liege*, which leads to
sacrilege, the stealing
of sacred things? The presentation

and movement of the cape to
attract, receive
and direct the charge of
the bull is called
pase. [. . .]¹⁰

Displaying an accumulated cache of the "sacred things" requires flirting with theft and sacrilege, just as the bullfighter's motions invite danger. The term *"pase,"* the present subjunctive of Spanish *pasar*, to pass, puts a spin of unknowability on the forms of language-gathering in which she works. When Estes presents a form of athletic or virtuosic choreography adjacent to an exploration of syntax, the juxtaposition suggests the simultaneous instability and potential of her own medium.

A volume replete with bodies in motion and phrases in flux, *Voice-Over* concludes with an elaborately choreographed elegiac dance. The penultimate poem, "Performance," which is followed only by the short coda "More," is set in the Oak Grove Cemetery in Delaware, Ohio, and presents a series of scenes or movements in arrays of stepwise triads, a form that recalls the later poems of William Carlos Williams:

The way fog speaks
            above the voice
                        of a river
or twenty Roman heads
            along a museum wall
                        look back
and call
            the one body
                        among them, torso
touching down
            lifting off
                        like a place,
I mean *plane*,
            trying to land
                        was the way
the possum lumbered
            toward us in the rain, [. . .]¹¹

The poem sets out to find an adequate metaphor for an unnamed grief, a way to articulate how "we are moved"—emotionally affected, set in motion. Reaching for metaphor in the natural world, then in the museum, then in the polysemy of "plane" as spatial field and mode of transport, Estes manipulates the indentations and enjambments to offer the phrases as choreographic annotations: "torso / touching down / lifting off." The body trails the train of thought, the cascading comparisons. The central encounter with a mother possum in the cemetery pivots abruptly on the word "she," evoking not the nocturnal creature but the unnamed performer of the title, and in so doing, announcing a straight-up metaphor: "She was an aria / in lilac fume, / heart-shaped, of course, / and beating / beneath a dress, lace / leaping / stage left / at the breast."[12] This complex image inscribes stage directions on the body, the phrases shifting indeterminately from source to source:

Recitative: *Whose cello first opened the air?*
Chorus: *The beech trees are wild*
with apostrophes.[13]

The chorus's line in this truncated script—this choreo-graph— suggests "apostrophe" as both direct address and typographic mark for possession or elision. Returning to the cemetery, the poem then regains its composure, gathering its wildness into lament:

They say it's not realistic—
        impossible, even—
                to sing
an aria while dying,
        and perhaps that's why
                we love
those scenes best:
        the last gasps,
                the highest
last and last,
        those mostly unreachable notes
                almost grasped
in the thin, last tightest breaths—
        how while lying
                motionless
we are moved
        the most—
                Is it sadness
or the relief of silence
        before a curtain
                falls,

rising again

        perhaps

                to applause.[14]

As the poem's phrases undulate and swing in waltz-form triplets, the impossibility of singing an aria while dying (or dancing while dying, for that matter) becomes an emblem for the urgency of the attempt. The aria with its "mostly unreachable notes" suggests a momentary stay against the inevitability of death, and the curtain falling on the performance becomes not closure but anticipation of another opening.

Awareness of the audience on the other side of the curtain allows this opening, a space that invites the viewer of the dance, and the reader of the poem, to respond with empathy and applause. Dance references in Estes's subsequent books are increasingly bound with elegy, the chorus-writing of dirge, and the movement of lament. In "Requiem," from *Chez Nous* (2005), we are reminded that "The origin of music was / grief."[15] The image of an animal killed on the road invokes a tragic performance:

> [. . .] how the hind leg rises
>
> at death, saluting
> the sky, just as at the end
>
> of Stravinsky's *Rite of*
> *Spring*, a girl steps onto
>
> the stage and dances herself
> to death. [. . .][16]

Dance in tragic forms is a mode of articulation of grief: in Stravinsky, a girl dances herself to death, underscoring in Estes's poem the finality of a corpse and a lost home. Yet Estes reminds us that dance can also function as elegy through more stylized and whimsical gestures. Elsewhere, an impending death seems to dance itself to life:

> [. . .] Before my father
> left the world, his blood looped out
>
> in tubes, orbiting his body
> the way the hem of Rita Hayworth's

black dress in *You'll Never*
Get Rich *circles her legs as they*

keep time with a pair of black
tuxedo slacks from a parallel universe

across a beach so bright it has turned
to glass. Fred Astaire sings *You're so near*

and yet so far, and they spin
as they dance their way offstage, lifting

and touching opposite arms overhead
like the arcs of skies that arrive and go away

while faces beneath them, like moons, remain.[17]

A dance image arises here from the fanciful imagining of the dying
father's blood as the hem of Rita Hayworth's skirt, the vehicle of a
metaphor that in turn vivifies a whole subsequent scene of roman-
tic performance, the line-breaks emphasizing elevation ("lifting,"
"overhead") and turning as the dancers inevitably separate. The fig-
ures in these poems are moving and moved, reminding us, as an-
other poem in *Chez Nous* does, that "to move / is always to bear /
change. . . ."[18]

As in *Voice-Over,* dance provides the finale of *Chez Nous,* another
expansive and annotated performance, "Dance of Ancient Knossos."
The poem begins in the imperative, with a directive for revivifying
the structures that underpin an elegiac or nostalgic stance toward
history: "Build a palace at Knossos, a labyrinth / from which there
is no / escape, if you want to hear the sound / of the past, although
there will be / no sound."[19] The poem revolves around quotations
from Satie's performance directions, from which Estes riffs and
meditates, arranging Satie's phrases with halting enjambments that
convey disjuncture of movement and thought: "*With the tip of your
thought. Postulate / within yourself. Step by / step. On the tongue.*"[20]
Estes manipulates Satie's language to embody—to give bodily form
and movement—to cognition:

And keep time
at the palace of *gnosis,* knowledge; let it lean
back like recognition, legs crossing over

and over while an *ostinato* bass
holds like stones beneath a current
of notes.[21]

Time is given a dancerly body, and the lineation enacts gesture and motion: "lean / back," and "legs crossing over / and over" hang time over the line-breaks, "bass" holds a moment of stillness, and the "current / of notes" turns and falls. Estes fully exploits what Giorgio Agamben calls the "schism of sound and sense," the rift he considers the defining trait of poetry—"the opposition of a metrical limit to a syntactical limit, of a prosodic pause to a semantic pause."[22] Estes stretches this verse ontology to include the spatial and proprioceptive tensions that arise in the verse line. Satie's directions take on gestural movement: "*Slow. Advise yourself carefully. Arm yourself / with clairvoyance. Alone for an instant. So that you obtain / a hollow.*"[23] Estes then invokes dance directly:

The river chants, looks
like a thread you could
follow—incantation without motif, "music
on one's knees," a Greek
dance performed right to
left, then left
to right, then stationary
before altar:[24]

That colon announces the inclusion of another graphic nomenclature, a printed portion of Satie's score, and these final instructions: "*Very lost. Carry that further. Open / your head. Bury the sound.*"[25] Agamben notes the ontological paradox that occurs at the end of a poem: if verse is defined by the turn of the furrow, the final line is "a decisive crisis," an "unexpected irruption of prose."[26] Estes's ending here seems both to ignore and to mourn that loss, to capitulate to that silence and stillness as a function of performative immediacy.

Tryst (2009) invites the reader directly into a dancerly performance space with its cover image—a dancer *en pointe*, in languorous *relevé*, wearing a 1956 costume by Tony Duquette, who figures as one of the collection's paradigmatic makers. Among Estes's books, *Tryst* is most indebted to a Terpsichoric muse, and it includes "*Bourrée*," where the Baroque dance of that name and the move in classical ballet become touchstones for an ars poetica:

At the opening of Act II
in *Giselle,* everyone dancing is
        dead or soon will be, and because
dancers pound new pointe shoes
        on the concrete to muffle the sound
made when they touch the floor,
        the Queen of the Wilis *bourrées*
across the stage without appearing
        to move her feet—like the hands
of a clock that say *six*, then *eight*,
        though we never see them shift, never
hear them speak.[27]

Citing a dance that forestalls tragic conclusion, Estes compares the dance step the *bourrée*, where rapid iteration of movements paradoxically creates the illusion of stillness, to the unwitnessed passage of time—the inevitable fact that an hour or a life elapses while we are absorbed in its particulars. The poem shifts among various scenes, as all Estes's poems do, from a photograph of her great-grandparents with their twelve children, to St. Erkenwald, to the recollection of her mother's toilette, which returns us to the body, and to dance as the vehicle of another metaphor:

[. . .] After her bath,
        my mother would paw the white
powder with her puff, then pat
        between her legs, beneath
her arms and breasts the way
        a ballerina's pointe shoes strike
the stage, deer running through
        duff in the forest or rain
hitting dust, on which, if your ear
        is close enough, you can hear
the rain pronounced.[28]

In this gorgeous conflation of sounds, the mother's ordinary bodily gesture suggests the sound of ballet shoes as objects, then the muffled sound of a wild animal, and finally, in a metaphorical leap that wraps back into its own linguistic medium, the sound of rain that speaks. The sonic pairing of "duff" and "dust," and "ear" and "hear," underscore auditory connections, and the perception of water droplets hitting dust suggests the poem's internal, percussive articulation. Like a dancer executing a series of *bourrée* steps to suggest gliding across a stage, Estes's mostly trimeter lines in "*Bourrée*" take a series of rapid steps in quick succession to carry the poem afield.

In *Tryst*, dance references are conduits of memory, aggregators of earlier forms and retrospective glances. "Olé" recalls "The Dance of the Sheets," where a dance practiced in a domestic not theatrical space elucidates dynamics between an observer and a dancer who might be mother and daughter:

> You are up on a table
> in the basement at night in your
> tap shoes, left arm bent, hand raised
> to the level of your head—a flamenco
> dancer ready to stamp and slap
> the fingers of the right hand
> to the cupped palm of
> the left: *olé.* If the taps
> on your shoes had cartoon
> balloons, they'd say *step,*
> *click, swoop, turn,*
> *click,* as if they were
> genes climbing their way up
> a strand of DNA with only five
> adjectives normally associated with
> machinery and the tune of *a thousand*
> *stars in the sky make me realize*
> to make them realize
> that the Delta 32 mutation can protect
> you and your descendants not only
> from the plague and from AIDS, but from
> your mother taking her X-ACTO knife
> voice to the strop of her tongue
> and saying *aha* that's what
> *I thought*, as she slaps your head
> with a rat-tail comb [. . .][29]

The poem traffics in the uncanniness of inheritance, exploring the fear and pain transmitted from parent to child, as well as the resilience—the Delta 32 mutation is an allele that allows HIV resistance. Here, watching dance entails an impulse to *caption* the steps, to have them utter their own choreography, a comic-strip recounting of the scene. The amateur tap dancer, precariously perched in the recesses of the house, models a pursuit of technique that is both humorous and chastening, the *olé* transmuted into the *aha* of remonstrance. *Olé*, the exclamation of encouragement customary in bullfights and flamenco, begins as cartoonish and stylized but then retrieves its origins in the Arabic *wa-llāh*, "and God," following the long tail of the past back to the atavistic dread of the dead returning. The speaker recalls the grandmother's superstitious fear of an eel in the pan coming back to life, and her shriek at seeing the speaker cross a room she had not noticed her enter, "as if I'd returned / from the dead."[30]

If choreography in *Tryst* is the embodiment of heredity, chorus-writing in *Enchantée* (2013) gestures toward the embodiment of history. The key figure in the capacious poem "History" is Loïe Fuller, whose interdisciplinary reach and flair for innovation among and through traditional forms suggest Estes's own. Pioneer of modern dance, costume design, and theatrical lighting, synthesizer of modes from vaudeville and burlesque into ballet, Fuller finds material in disparate sources. Their layered convergence, as in Estes's work, becomes an opportunity for exploring and documenting movement and improvisation, for creating and framing what we experience as "space":

> Mallarmé said that Loie Fuller, with the wing
> of her skirt, created space
> like the new convertible
> brought home by the neighbors
> on our block: at first a question mark
> in the sky, then rising above them
> half a parenthesis until only
> a comma was left behind, the shape
> of their hands as they waved
> down the street. "We ought to say a feeling
> of *and,* a feeling of *if,* a feeling of
> *but,* and a feeling of *by,*" William James
> claimed, "quite as readily as we say
> a feeling of blue or a feeling
> of cold," [. . .][31]

Laden with prepositions rather than modifiers, the passage evokes positionality line by line. Shapes arise within the anecdote—the lexical suggestiveness of the contours of objects like "commas," for example—and also within the field of the page, with its irregular indentations. Line-breaks on "only" and "waved" suggest falling and turning, then the James quotation underscores the proprioceptive apprehension of adjacency (by), contingency (if), and connection (and). Estes's improvisatory spacing frames absences and syntactic hinges, drawing attention to the junctures where accounts—histories—have not yet solidified as fact or truth:

> [. . .] The empty spaces, Conrad
> said of maps, are the most
> interesting places because they are
> what will change.[32]

"History" reminds us that space is created, fabricated, that we do not see it as space until it is defined and demarcated by what is not space but object—by not-space, by the body. The poem returns to the complex visual image created by the motion of the car's convertible top, and then to the body's role at the root of remembering:

> [. . .] to remember
> in Spanish, *recorder,* means to pass
> once more through the heart
> the way the blood keeps coming
> back for another tour, another
> spin around the block. The yellow-
> orange sash flapping past the window
> was memorable, a memorial, so much
> like an oriole or the scarf that keeps
> circling the past's held
> note: [. . .][33]

Estes reminds us that memory, in its etymological history, is a "circulatory system," a means of moving energy through the body, arising from the re-cording heart. Her imagery transmutes body to space to landscape, as the blood in circulation in turn suggests the car's movement around the neighborhood streets. The metaphorical cascade of "History" finds its way in and out of choreography and physiology, much in the same way that the dying father's blood in "So Near Yet So Far" suggests the swirl of Rita Hayworth's dress. Ultimately, as in the elegiac dance poems of earlier books, the shapes of space and the movements in air return the audience, the observer, to the finality of death. The "memorable" orange sash reminds us that Fuller's great protégé, Isadora Duncan, lost her life when one of her flowing scarves, caught on the axle of an Amilcar, broke her neck.

Dance braids itself into Estes's poems among countless other allusions, definitions, associative flights, touchstones, tangents. Dance images are perhaps less apparent to her readers than her references to visual and literary culture, but also perhaps more structurally germane, more intrinsic to her understanding of the forms of poetry. Estes's engagement with dance and dancers spans five books, not only as source of comparison and imagery, but as figures for movement, lineation, pacing, extension, and juxtaposition. This much-quoted passage from "Ars Poetica" in *Enchantée* resonates with many readers as a summary gesture of Estes's poetics, but the way it places dance at the center of an understanding of her oeuvre remains unremarked. The quintessential Baroque word, dreamed here, appears as a corps of dancers:

> I once dreamed a word entirely
> Baroque: a serpentine line of letters leaning
> with the flourish of each touching the shoulder
> of another so that one breath at the word's
> beginning made them all collapse [. . .][34]

The word "serpentine," in a volume where Loïe Fuller appears, gestures toward Fuller's most famous dance, the 1891 serpentine dance—the word is a brief oneiric glimpse of performative space. The fundamental units of Estes's own medium—a line of letters—is figured as a chorus-line of dancers, shoulder to shoulder, bodies in space rehearsing a unified fall. Language, literalized as a chorus, collapses with the body's breath. The lines enact what choreographers call a controlled transference of weight, the coordination of gravitational pull and counter-stance, the collapse as signifier, transmitting meaning in the fall. Estes's apotheosis of the Baroque word, dreamed as a line of dancers, gives way to the local habitation of bodies in space as they dramatize capitulation to time.

Works Cited

Agamben, Giorgio. "The End of the Line." In *The Lyric Theory Reader*, ed. Virginia Jackson and Yopie Prins. Baltimore: Johns Hopkins University Press, 2014.
Estes, Angie. *Chez Nous*. Oberlin: Oberlin College Press, 2005.
Estes, Angie. *Enchantée*. Oberlin: Oberlin College Press, 2013.

Estes, Angie. *Tryst.* Oberlin: Oberlin College Press, 2009.

Estes, Angie. *The Uses of Passion.* Salt Lake City: Gibbs Smith, 1995.

Estes, Angie. *Voice-Over.* Oberlin: Oberlin College Press, 2002.

Lesser, Wendy. "The Diction of Dance: Applying Poetics to Dance: A Review of the Recent New York Dance Season." *Poetry Foundation* (February 7, 2006). Online. Available at https://www.poetryfoundation.org/features/articles/detail/68466

Notes

1. Angie Estes. *Enchantée* (Oberlin: Oberlin College Press, 2013), 7.
2. Ibid., 8.
3. Angie Estes. *Chez Nous* (Oberlin: Oberlin College Press, 2005), 27.
4. Estes, *Enchantée*, 1.
5. Wendy Lesser. "The Diction of Dance: Applying Poetics to Dance: A Review of the Recent New York Dance Season." *Poetry Foundation,* February 7, 2006. Online. Available at https://www.poetryfoundation.org/features/articles/detail/68466
6. Angie Estes. *The Uses of Passion* (Salt Lake City: Gibbs Smith, 1995), 23.
7. Ibid., 23.
8. Angie Estes. *Voice-Over* (Oberlin: Oberlin College Press, 2002), 36.
9. Estes, *Chez Nous*, 15.
10. Estes, *Voice-Over*, 29–30.
11. Ibid., 62.
12. Ibid., 62.
13. Ibid., 63.
14. Ibid., 63.
15. Estes, *Chez Nous*, 34.
16. Ibid., 33.
17. Angie Estes. *Tryst* (Oberlin: Oberlin College Press, 2009), 60–61.
18. Estes, *Chez Nous*, 42.
19. Ibid., 68.
20. Ibid., 68.
21. Ibid., 68.
22. Giorgio Agamben. "The End of the Line." In *The Lyric Theory Reader,* ed. Virginia Jackson and Yopie Prins (Baltimore: Johns Hopkins University Press, 2014), 431, 430.
23. Estes, *Chez Nous*, 68.
24. Ibid., 68.
25. Ibid., 69.
26. Agamben, "The End of the Line," 432.
27. Estes, *Tryst*, 37.
28. Ibid., 37–38.
29. Ibid., 42.
30. Ibid., 43.

31. Estes, *Enchantée*, 13.
32. Ibid., 13.
33. Ibid., 14.
34. Ibid., 56.

DOUG RUTLEDGE

"*Visibile Parlare*"
Ekphrastic Images in the Poetry of Angie Estes

Angie Estes is one of the most ekphrastic of contemporary American poets. However, because she is not writing narrative poetry, she challenges conventional theories of ekphrastic art. For example, Stephen Cheeke argues that "the division between the rhetoric of art criticism and the poetry of ekphrasis is only a matter of degree."[1] Cheeke's observation would imply that the goal of ekphrastic poetry is to clarify the unnoticed or the unsaid in visual art. Yet that implication runs counter to the way art is employed in much of contemporary poetry. In spite of the fact that Estes's poetry uses the term "*visibile parlare*,"[2] and often describes talking paintings, she is not trying to write poetry that simply speaks for the mute art works she references. Therefore, when Heffernan describes ekphrasis as "*a verbal representation of a pictorial representation*"[3] (emphasis in original), he oversimplifies the way a contemporary poet like Estes is employing art. Estes uses works of art as images in lyric poems that are pointedly avoiding the narrative structure that Cheeke's observation and Heffernan's definition would imply. In a recent essay, Stephanie Burt refers to Estes's poetry as "nearly Baroque," asserting that "Estes's imagined motions, the serpentine curves of her irregular lines, take her not only from artwork to artwork but also from place to place, stitching together in her imagination . . ."[4] several complex images. The point is Estes uses art in intricate metaphors that are doing much more than simply translating or speaking for paintings, architecture, sculpture, or photographs.

It is true that Heffernan complicates his position to some extent by saying that "ekphrasis speaks not only *about* works of art but also *to* and *for* them. In so doing, it stages—within the theatre of language itself—a revolution of the image against the word . . ."[5] (emphasis in original). Certainly, Estes's poetry is engaging in a dialogue with works of visual art. However, Heffernan goes on to assert that "ekphrasis . . . is a literary mode that turns on antagonism. . . ."[6] For

Estes, the notion of antagonism between art and poetry is itself antagonistic to what she is trying to accomplish. The relationship between poetic and physical art is much more like teamwork for her. In fact, Estes employs artistic images as a way of cooperating with visual works of art to accomplish what might be described as a mutually agreed upon goal of moving an audience between one state of being and another.

Estes has said that she distrusts the narrative in poetry. Instead, she "think[s] of a poem as . . . filled with 'divine details,' and the poem is an arranged place—like the golden chalices, rubies, emeralds, and stained glass windows of Abbot Suger's chapel—where experience happens" (Dialogue; this volume, p. 69). Suger was an advocate of using art to inspire awe. As Honorius of Atun explained, "pictures were the literature of the laity."[7] So when Estes refers to Suget in "Rebus," the poem and the Abbot are working together to achieve emotional uplift in the poem's audience. Estes often refers to Dante in her poetry and claims, "I have been doing a kind of medieval, anagogical thinking most of my life" (Dialogue, p. 68). In "Pietà," Estes writes, "the highest form of divine / communication Dante calls *visibile / parlare,* visible speaking. . . ."[8] In the poem named for the artist's sculpture, both Michelangelo and Estes are engaged in *visibile parlare*; they are both using the image of Mary mourning for her dead son to speak visibly to audiences, to raise them to an emotional height where didacticism is unnecessary.

Our primary source for the hermeneutical practice of anagogy comes from Dante's Letter to Con Grande where the poet explains that the literal and historical interpretations of an event are contained within the letter. Even on the literal level then, words as objects are charged with meaning. However, sometimes objects and events remind us of a larger story, and sometimes they do so in a transcendent fashion. Dante calls the anagogical level mysterious, but by that he seems to refer to the divine metaphor. In other words, the historical moment when the people of Israel escape from Egypt is a representation on the anagogical level of the "leave taking of the blessed soul from the slavery of this corruption to the freedom of eternal glory."[9] More than metaphor, however, the poet implies that all objects and events are charged with meaning beyond themselves, meaning, which as Estes asserts, leads from one world, one state of being, to another and is alive to the engaged mind (see Dialogue, pp. 68–69).

In her first book, *The Uses of Passion,* Estes explores the idea that poetry might speak for mute works of art, but while doing so she moves beyond that notion to work with the art object toward a sense of shared meaning. Her poems complicate the vision presented by the painting by bringing other images and experiences to the poetic response to the visual work of art. Because of Estes's ekphrastic subject in "Giotto's Last Judgment," there is no difference between the literal and the anagogical, or as the speaker puts it, "in his painting / there is little or no distinction / between the human and the divine."[10] This is not true of the poem, however, which contains used carpet salesmen and senior yearbooks. Because Giotto does not employ the Renaissance practice of perspective, the poet explains that "In rapture," the two-dimensional elect "do not know that they are almost // an artistic failure."[11] The two dimensions of this fresco are similar to the dual dimensions of the earthly and the divine that operate throughout the poem and the art work, for just as Giotto's "Last Judgment" portrays the saved and the damned, so the poem compares the angel recounting history to a "used carpet salesman [explaining] how passion / first spilled onto life like a stain / and then stayed indistinguishable // from the color of the fabric itself."[12] The play on the word passion introduces a theme of divine and earthly love, which is both in the fresco and outside of it.

The angels go on to demonstrate that they are in fact an artistic success, because

Giotto's fresco lets the angel give
one last pitch: everything,

he continues to insist, reminds us
of something else, points
to something beyond

its own name: the way a spot
on the heart's monitor leaps once
and then lies flat forever

and absence, thin as air,
left alone long enough
turns to flame.[13]

The notion that everything reminds us of something else is a medieval aesthetic, recalling Dante's letter to Con Grande, so it implies a movement from the historical or literal level outside the painting to the anagogical level within it. There is no doubt that this is Dante's *visibile parlare*, or as Estes quotes Voltaire in "*Le Plaisir*," "*l'écriture est la peinture de la / voix*."[14] The painting is developing a voice.

However, even in this early work Estes insists on doing more than simply describing the work of art as if she were an art critic. The fresco is like everything else in the poet's experience. It reminds her of something higher, but it also reminds her of very earthly objects outside the painting itself: a carpet salesman, a yearbook, a heart monitor, and the absence of love. The movement to the higher state of being represented by Giotto's work requires some very earthly experiences that the speaker and other members of the fresco's audience bring to the experience of viewing it.

"St. Francis Preaching to the Birds" is another response to Giotto and also a poem that is interested in thinking about how art might achieve speech, though the poem does not think of itself as simply speaking for the fresco. In spite of the poem's title, it asserts that "no one / in the painting speaks."[15] Yet the painting moves from the literal to the anagogical with the structural elements of language:

> So far, only one thing reaches
> toward heaven, a tree whose spine curves
> behind them like a comma, and in the space it frames
> at the center of the painting is a pause
> on which an evening grosbeak and a pigeon
> still intend to land.[16]

The comma here signifies a silent speech, which reifies itself to the extent that it creates physical space on which the birds can land. This dichotomy of silent speech occurring within art appears again when St. Francis becomes an artist within the fresco or at least within the poet's imaginary view of it:

> St. Francis drew them
> a picture of the hole in the ground
>
> where what was once the ground
> used to be, and without speaking a word
> before he turned to leave said, *Let us*
> *pray to this place that is not*
> *a place, let the three toes*
> *of this tree hold on*

while the gold flecks of the sky
peel back; let us believe that we can say
what it will be like to stay put:
at first a flock of bushtits, nipping
at the heart; then overhead,
the unaccountable stars.[17]

We are in a place that is no place, where the physical can become language and language can become tangible. Here, without speaking a word, St. Francis is able to talk to the birds and pray for them, as he prays for transcendence. Just as Giotto's painting is meant to move his audience from their physical, historical space to the anagogical space St. Francis represents, so in the poem St. Francis imagines for the birds a sky, where gold flecks peel back to reveal "unaccountable stars." The Saint and his image comfort the birds, while lifting his audience, the audience of the painting and the audience of the poem, to a higher level.

In her later books, Estes's use of ekphrasis becomes considerably more complex. *Tryst*'s "Takeoff" is a good example of a poem in which she employs visual works of art as images to make a larger thematic point. The title of the poem offers a hint of its theme. The poet is concerned with emotional uplift and specifically the kind that comes from love. Throughout the poem, Estes is interested in both divine and earthly love. This is indicated by Camille Saint-Saëns's *Samson and Delilah* in which Delilah sings to Samson that her "*heart opens at* [his] *voice*,"[18] and yet she will betray him because of his loyalty to *Yahweh*. Earthy love is also referenced by the lover in the poem's frame, who is taking off on a plane, and the lifting up that occurs during sexual climax at the end of the poem.

Estes calls on two paintings to help her develop the theme of divine and earthly love in "Takeoff." The first is Fra Angelico's painting of the Saints Cosme and Damien. Before becoming third-century martyrs, these men were doctors, who, according to legend, cared for the poor. Their spiritual form of love is described by the Latin word, *caritas*, or charity. When Cosme and Damien refused to deny their Christian faith, they were stoned, hung on a cross, shot with arrows, and beheaded. Here, the central image of "Takeoff" becomes considerably more complicated. Unlike the lover, who is flying away and whose body arches during sexual consummation, this uplift requires bloody sacrifice. Moreover, the poet seems to suggest that the appropriate response is reified by the trees:

> In Fra Angelico's painting, even the flames
> of cypress flare up
> along the road where the gold-haloed
> heads of the martyred Saints Cosme and Damien
> roll like rocks with notes
> bound over their eyes. [19]

The trees are a central image of the painting; they lift the viewer's eye away from the rolling heads toward the sky, suggesting what the sacrifice of Cosme and Damien achieved. The love represented by their charity has been transformed into divine love through sacrifice. It is noteworthy that the painting is set in a medieval, not a classical Roman, mise-en-scène, suggesting that the sacrifice of the martyrs is eternal and ongoing in the world of the poet as well as that of the painter.

Immediately, the poet employs the image of the cypress trees to move the emotional sacrifice and uplift they evoke to a more contemporary moment:

> *It is a splash*
> *of black in a sunny landscape,*
> van Gogh said of the cypress,
> *but it is one of the most interesting*
> *black notes, and the most difficult*
> *to hit off that I can*
> *imagine.*[20]

Here, Estes is quoting from a letter van Gogh wrote to his brother Theo on June 25, 1889. The painting to which the quote refers is entitled "Cypresses" and was painted in late June of that year. As the passage suggests, the trees are in the middle of a sunny landscape. They create a play between light and dark, but they also offer the eyes visual direction, as they did in Fra Angelico's painting. Of course, the cypress tree, like the church steeple, fulfills much the same purpose in another work van Gogh painted in June of 1889, "Starry Night." Here the play between earth and heaven as well as the emotional uplift would seem closer to what Fra Angelico intended to evoke. It is interesting to reflect on the fact that these works were created the year after van Gogh cut off his ear, a physical mutilation, which is not entirely dissimilar from the sacrifice that Cosme and Damien chose to make. Moreover, as van Gogh used that ear to pay a prostitute, the interaction between divine and earthly love continues to play out here, though perhaps in an ironic fashion.

In *Enchantée*, this theme of moving from one state of being to another is often evoked through paintings involving birds. For example, "One Speaks of Divine Things on a Sky-Blue Field" references a medieval saint and his birds in a complex manner that also involves medieval poetry:

> as the birds fly in to hear
> St. Francis speak in Giotto's fresco, their bodies turning
> transparent before they touch the ground
> so the blue sky beyond them
> can be seen: *sweet color*
>
> *of oriental sapphire* that spread
> above Dante as he climbed up out of Hell. . . .[21]

This very stunning moment, in which the evening sky opens up as Dante climbs out of the dark and stench-filled bowels of hell, is evoked here to suggest the movement to a higher state of being Estes's poetry often struggles to achieve. But the elevated state is also represented in the fresco by the birds and by Saint Francis who cares for them, so that once again, painting and poetry are working together in a kind of *visibile parlare* designed to lift their audience from one state of being to another.

In a complex and comic manner, Estes's interest in ekphrastic poetry is also evoked in *Tryst*'s "First Life of St. Francis." This poem refers to painting, opera, and photography; it comments on art history and perspective, but its use of ekphrasis is especially complex, so that the work of art at the heart of the poem brings together and makes physical an intricate and interwoven series of themes and ideas.

The poem has the tone, if not the structure, of Jabberwocky or fairy tale, but its intentional play with what seems like nonsense has a theme of using art to move between one world and another. Perhaps that is why, very early in the poem, the poet tells us that St. Francis seemed "like a new Manet, one from another / work of art."[22] The central image of the poem, the event that occurs on the literal level, involves the story of St. Francis picking up worms and moving them off of paths, so they would not be stepped on. In its first telling, we can make out the story through the syntax, though the words themselves have something else entirely to say:

> Therefore, whenever he would find
> anything writhing, whether goddess or
> *mañana*, along the waves, or in a hover of *how
> do you do*, or on a flounce, he would pick it up
> with the greatest revision and put it in a sad
> or deciduous place, so that nameless loot
> would not rename *there* or anything else
> rain could do.[23]

The theme of worms repeats itself and becomes more evident as the poem goes on, but at first it seems difficult to associate these writhings with that creature, as it squirms back and forth across the soil. While one has to be careful about overreading such a passage, words like "revision" and "rename" suggest a theme of writing. This theme becomes confusingly more intense as the passage continues:

> One day when he was asked
> by a certain bother why he so diligently
> picked up writhings even of Paganini
> or writhings in which there was no mercy
> for nay-saying at Lourdes, he replied,
> *Syllables are the litter out of which the most
> glorious neighing of the Lord God
> covers the earth: they burnish
> the gold leaf lores of the white-throated
> sparrow and lie along the highway, bob
> on canals unmentioned but by goldfinches
> alone, to whom belong every gondola.*[24]

In spite of our earlier association of the passage with worms, the writhing has become writing, which belongs to Paganini as music or lyrics, but also to the Lord God as neighing syllables. What is interesting here, however, is that language does for us the same thing that the humility of St. Francis, expressed in his care for animals, does for him: it moves him from a pedestrian to an elevated state, just as the worm is moved from danger to safety.

The poet then seems to joke with us about the worm trick:

The presence of worms in the odd song lyrics (songs,
poems, operas) is a fact: what to do with this and
how to interpret it?[25]

How to interpret is certainly the question with which this poem presents us. In the next section, the theme of transcendence becomes reified in art, in the halos within art, in picture frames, and finally in the speaker's memory of fishing with worms:

> But as artists developed
> perspective, halos were tilted, hollowed,
> made transparent until da Vinci
> eliminated them altogether. Some claim,
> however, that halos did not disappear
> but became disguised
> as hats or arches: in *The Last Supper,*
> above Christ's head an arch
> appears, while Vermeer in the background
> of his paintings hangs square
> picture frames as halos. Above me
> is a framed photograph of a river
> I used to fish, but was it a kind
> of virtue to lift a rainbow
> trout from the stream, interrupt
> its spurt and hurry, and slit
> its silver seam—pull out
> the red and blue, sometimes
> a bit of green—and leave it looking
> as if it still intended
> to swim?[26]

Here, in a concrete fashion, the poet has shown us how art moves us from one world, one state of being to another. People in art become a saint with the addition of a halo, an arch or even a picture frame. And the transformation can occur outside of physical art as well, as the poet, herself, has a picture frame over her head, as if she were the sacred person in Vermeer's painting. This is a very complex and sophisticated use of ekphrasis. For the picture over the poet causes her to move from one world to another again, when she remembers the act of fishing on the river portrayed in the photograph.

This memory establishes dramatic tension, as the poet does not protect her animals, the fish and its bait, as St. Francis would have. Instead she slits the fish's "silver seam" and asks herself if that were the virtuous thing to do. This difference between St. Francis and the poet meditating upon him is extended as the speaker considers the difference between how she treated her worm and how St. Francis treated them:

> I had to push
> a hook into the worm's thick
> girdle, feel it writhe inside
> my hand like a girlfriend's finger
> spelling out words
> on my palm in the darkened
> room during school movies. Another loop
> and puncture, loop and stick, almost
> knitting, until only the last inch
> like the tail of a *y* swayed
> below the hook. *Toward*
> *little worms even, Saint Francis glowed*
> *with a very great love, for he had read*
> *this saying about the Savior:* "I am
> a worm, not a man." *Therefore he picked them*
> *up from the road and placed them*
> *in a safe place, lest they be crushed*
> *by the feet of the passersby.* He knew their
> favorite opera, *Rigoletto,* how they
> pass their soft bodies
> through the earth, carving,
> as they go, their own
> round halos.[27]

Here the dramatic tension between the speaker and St. Francis is accentuated, as she finally gets around to clearly revealing the mysterious story of St. Francis and the worms. Notice, as the speaker tells us her story of putting the worm onto the hook, she does so with two or perhaps three forms of art as metaphor: knitting, the writing her girlfriend performs on her palm, and the movie. Art within art moves us between worlds, as the poet slays, even as St. Francis saves, the worms.

Religion, in the person of St. Francis, moves the worms between worlds, or at least between safe and dangerous places, but art moves them too. After all, St. Francis knows their favorite opera, "Rigoletto." The speaker warned us earlier that worms appear in opera librettos. Certainly that is true of "Rigoletto," if we hold with the tradition that serpents are also called worms. For when the Count of Monterone curses Rigoletto in Act I, he says:

E tu, serpente,
tu che d'un padre ridi al dolore,
sii maledetto!

[and you, you serpent,
you who ridicule a father's grief,
my curse upon you!][28]

The worms also like this opera, because of the "o"s in Rigoletto's name, which are like the halos the worms create for themselves as they crawl beneath the ground. The photograph and references to the works of Leonardo da Vinci and Vermeer make "The First Life of St. Francis" an ekphrastic poem, but it seems safe to say that the poem is doing much more than simply speaking for a silent work of art.

Estes's poem "Ars Poetica" speaks of the divine energy in works of art. Here, she cites Leonardo da Vinci's theory of art, which "sought / to reconcile the apparent contradiction / between a static, lifeless / artifact and the enlivenment / it provokes. . . ."[29] He accomplishes this by suggesting that "art must be / measured by its *vivacità*. . . ."[30] This notion of vivifying a work of art is very much in evidence in her poem "Here Lightning has Been," a poem that is ekphrastic at its core, because its central image is a photograph. The poem's first stanza recalls the ancient Roman notion that anything touched by lightning has been infused with the energy of god. Next the poem cites Plutarch to assert that human bodies can absorb divine power when touched by lightning. Subsequently, the speaker associates this kind of divine energy with writing and dance:

In his diary,
Nijinsky wrote that he had
invented a fountain pen
called God: *Handwriting*
is a beautiful thing,
and therefore it must be
preserved.[31]

Writing is infused, but as the poem is referencing Nijinsky, it seems to imply that dance can be similarly energized. Toward the end of the poem, the speaker attributes this energy, this meaning, this beauty to art. Moreover, she does this in a particularly ekphrastic manner, in that she is interpreting a photograph, so that the dance, the picture of the dancer, and the poem describing him are all infused with a special kind of energy:

> In 1939, after shock
> treatments, Nijinsky was visited
> by photographers who asked to see
> his famous leap. In one picture
> Nijinsky appears—in dark
> jacket, trousers, and shoes—highlighted
> against a white wall, a foot
> and a half above the floor, arms
> outstretched and blurred like a hummingbird
> hovering at a flower or a man before
> a firing squad at close range,
> > > each sip a *jeté*
> of light.[32]

The shock treatment is analogous to Jupiter's lightning bolt in that it infuses the artist with energy. The shock treatment occurs on the literal level, but the divine leap, which transforms a mentally ill man into an artist, could be said to be operating on the anagogical level. The *jeté* of light reminds us of the lightning of the first stanza, but it is also what the stained-glass windows created in Abbot Suger's St. Denis.

However, the poem is larger than Nijinsky, for the poet is telling us how art works for her. The objects about which the poet writes are infused with energy. The linguistic structure contains that energy, so that the energy and the meaning are within the poem itself. Finally, the energy and the meaning make the art transcendent, like Nijinsky's leap.

Estes often employs architectural imagery to inspire this movement from one state of being to another, but she does this in a complex manner, so she is never simply describing visual works of art. In "Rebus," the Latin word for "things" and the title of a poem in *Voice-Over*, the speaker tells us how

           Abbot Suger
in twelfth-century   France
       arranged   topaz jasper
sapphire   onyx   on the altar
       of the Abbey of St. Denis   placed
gold and silver   chalices
                to catch   divine light
like a line drive to first. . . .[33]

Abbott Suger was a major intellectual force behind the movement
from Romanesque to Gothic architecture. He was also a major in-
fluence behind the rebuilding of St. Denis and of Chartres Cathe-
dral. Gothic architecture is designed to let more light into the sa-
cred space, an idea based on Longinus's notion of the sublime and
the neo-Platonist influence on the twelfth-century Renaissance.

   Chez Nous considers architecture throughout the book. In
"*Rendez-Vous*," the poet begins by considering the sculpture of St.
Teresa by Bernini, which is famously surrounded by streams of di-
vine light. Then the speaker asks:

       . . . is it architecture, sculpture
in the round, relief? *In my Father's house
are many mansions,* the many-chambered rose
religieuse. . . .[34]

The many-mansioned house is heaven, of course, as Christ de-
scribes it in the Gospel of John, but it is also a medieval cathedral,
the chambered rose, where we might see stained glass and experi-
ence another twist on medieval aesthetics and ontology, as we do in
"*Vis-À-Vis*":

       Her skin, stained-

glass window, each pane
opaque and leaded
with light around its edges, we call

hide, we call *stepping stones to
heaven: Notre Dame de la Belle
Verrière,* Our Lady of the Beautiful

Window, *for now we see through a glass,
darkly.* . . .[35]

The cathedral encloses both divine and earthly space, both literal and anagogical, for in it we are surrounded by the divine light represented by stained glass, and yet it is still a place where we see through a glass darkly.

It is interesting to think that the many-mansioned house is also *Chez Nous,* both "our house" and the book itself. However, *chez nous* is also a place where we still see through a glass darkly and where art has no voice:

> . . . but *chez nous*
> the paintings have
> no mouths and do not need
> to sing because what we call
> darkness darkens
> in octaves.[36]

The poem employs images from paintings by Sargent, Haydn's *Farewell Symphony,* and architecture by Palladio:

> According to Sargent,
> a portrait is a painting
> with something wrong with
> the mouth . . .

> *And indeed,*
> *if we consider this beautiful*
> *machine of the world,*
> Palladio wrote, so much needs
> Oiling. . . .[37]

In keeping with the theme that *Chez Nous* is a many-mansioned house, like a cathedral, it is interesting to note that Palladio, the architect, was writing about how this world needs more temples:

> If we consider this beautiful machine of the world . . . we cannot
>   doubt, but that
> the little temples we make ought to resemble this great one,
>   which, by his
> immense goodness, was perfectly compleated by one word of his.[38]

In many ways *Chez Nous* is like this temple, a house of many mansions, built according to the need declared by Archbishop Suget to let in more light, so the book of that title is complete with stained glass windows of Notre Dame and Bernini's sculpture of St. Teresa. It also has its own aesthetic apocalypse:

> *Chez Nous*
> the world will end
> like the end of Haydn's *Farwell*
> *Symphony*, when all the players,
> one by one, get up
> from their seats and walk
> offstage.[39]

Painting and medieval architecture in the form of Chartres appear in a very complex fashion in Estes's poem "Entrance to an Imaginary Villa." The speaker opens the poem by restating the theme of transcendence, which is so important to her, and speaks of the way this movement to a higher state of being is manipulated by art:

> How easily the edge
> of this world becomes
> the edge of the next,
> the way the bedroom wall
> of the Villa Fanius
> at Boscoreale is a painting
> of the entrance
> to a villa whose third
> and fourth stories hang
> in verdigris air, impossible
> to reach from here.[40]

Here art seems to be a temptation, promising an entrance into another world and then removing the possibility as soon as it presents itself. However, the speaker quickly redefines—indeed reifies—the nature of imaginary space, so that no-place becomes someplace and the impossible transition possible:

> Is there a room . . .
>> It could be the home
> of memory, no place,
> the room where Augustine
> finally found God, and it hangs
> in the shade with nothing
> but room to grow, room

for error, which lives there as light
lives on in the cathedral
of Chartres at night. *Open
and close me,* Augustine prayed,
*like a vowel, like a window
with no view.*[41]

This complex and lovely metaphor recalls a famous one from John Donne. We began with the image of a room that does not exist and a promise of transcendence that cannot materialize, and then, as in "The Canonization," we move to an imaginary room, a room that is a state of mind, "the home of memory," which for Augustine's transcendence is more important than the physical room or moving between rooms in physical space. Again, we are moving between Dante's literal and anagogical levels. The reader, like the poem itself, begins in a room and ends in a transcendent space that is everywhere and nowhere. Augustine's home of memory is reified in Chartres, where transcendence is made real by the magnificent outburst of light. Finally, and most magnificently, Augustine himself is transformed into language, language like the Word, that can be opened, "like a vowel, like a window with no view."

"Per Your Request," the first poem in *Enchantée*, employs both pagan and Christian architecture to invoke the transition between the earthly and the transcendent. It is also a poem about divine and earthly love. The poem begins with a reference to the oculus of the Pantheon and its gilded bronze rosettes. The oculus is important, because it does not hold the viewer in the building but releases her to the heavens. The dome is like the poem itself, inspiring its readers to ascend, to move from one emotional, even spiritual, state of being to another.

gilded bronze rosettes once pressed
through the Pantheon's dome like stars

filling the coffers of the sky,
and history posed especially

for you, its spree become
repose. From the Janiculum hill

across the Tiber, you watched
the aureole settle around

its nipple as if a flying saucer
nestled among the rising

stones. . . .[42]

The Pantheon is dedicated to all of the gods, and the poem
seems to share that concept with the building. We move from the
Pantheon to the Janiculum hill. As the *Aeneid* tells us, the Janiculum
has always been the spiritual center of Rome. It is dedicated to Ja-
nus, the god who looks both ways, the god of new beginnings.

As we move to the Janiculum hill, we are introduced to the
"you" of the poem. Does the "you" represent the poet's new begin-
ning? Certainly, in that this is the first poem of a book, it does, but
are there other ways in which this might be a new beginning? The
fact that the view from the Janiculum hill down onto the Pantheon
becomes a nipple adds sexual connotations to the new start. The
literal dimension of the aureole here might be clouds encircling the
temple, though it could also refer to the circle around the nipple of
a human breast. An aureole is also a crown, and a halo, the god-like
aurora that surrounds saints in medieval paintings. So we are given
at once sexual and mystical connotations of the experience, divine
and human love once again.

As the poem continues, it evokes more architectural images of
transition.

Wisteria still hopes

over every wall, holding it
in place, while the lantern of Sant'Ivo

screws into the sky. When the snakes
sacred to Asclepius arrived

on Isola Tiberina, they made themselves
at home on the floors of the temple

dedicated to healing. . . .[43]

Wisteria is a flower of transitions. It represents the door between
the mortal world and that of the gods, so it is appropriate that the

poem associates wisteria with the Baroque masterpiece, the church of Sant'Ivo. As the poem suggests, the lantern of this church has the appearance of a corkscrew, as if the uppermost part of the church were trying to screw itself into the heavens in order to have physical contact with the divine.

Sant'Ivo screwing itself into the sky above Rome reifies the emotional movement of the poem, which is also made literal by the oculus of the Pantheon, and which in turn reifies a movement from the literal to the anagogical, the physical existence in the building and the spiritual existence represented by the oculus.

We then move back to the Roman Pantheon with Asclepius, the god of medicine and health. The *Isola Tibernia*, the island of the Tiber, is the home of Asclepius's temple. While Rome was suffering from an outbreak of the plague, a delegation was charged by the Senate to create a temple to Asclepius. During the search for an appropriate location for the temple, a snake, which had wrapped itself around the mast of the delegation's ship, swam to the island. This was considered a good omen. Asclepius represents the transition from illness to health. The speaker of the poem and her "you" could be healing from a past and moving to a future. "Per Your Request" is a poem about divine and earthly love. Temples represent divine uplift, but by the time the poem ends, with the "posse of roses coming / to possess you," the roses represent an earthly love that was earlier evoked by the sexual connotations surrounding the divine oculus of the Pantheon and its bronze rosettes.

Throughout Estes's six books of poetry, then, she often employs visual works of art as images in her poems. However, she never employs her poetic discourse in the way an art critic would. She does not simply explain the movement or the meaning of art works. Instead she attempts to work with pieces of art and their artists to create an emotional response similar to that which the work of art originally inspired. In her imagistic poetry, Estes uses visual works of art and other images to move her audience from one emotional state, one state of being, to another. Medieval art, a cathedral, or even shock treatment are among the things that might transform people and that seem to Estes images that aid her poetry in achieving her aesthetic goal. As we have seen, for Estes, words themselves are charged objects on the literal level, but they can be transformed to the anagogical by a dialectical arrangement between visual art and poetry that takes us through the doors of our minds, where with a small stroke of light, we can all learn to leap.

Works Cited

Alighieri, Dante. "Letter to Con Grande," trans. James Marchand. Georgetown University. Online. Accessed March 29, 2014.

Burt, Stephanie. "Nearly Baroque." *The Boston Review* (March/April 2014): 63–71.

Cheeke, Stephen. *Writing for Art: The Aesthetics of Ekphrasis*. Manchester, UK: Manchester University Press, 2008.

Eco, Umberto. *Art and Beauty in the Middle Ages*, trans. Hugh Bredin. New Haven: Yale University Press, 1986.

Estes, Angie. *Chez Nous*. Oberlin: Oberlin College Press, 2005.

Estes, Angie. *Enchantée*. Oberlin: Oberlin College Press, 2013.

Estes, Angie. *Tryst*. Oberlin: Oberlin College Press, 2009.

Estes, Angie. *The Uses of Passion*. Salt Lake City: Gibbs Smith, 1995.

Estes, Angie. *Voice-Over*. Oberlin: Oberlin College Press, 2002.

Estes, Angie, and Karen Rigby. "Means of Transport, Medieval Mind: A Dialogue with Angie Estes." *Cerise Press: A Journal of Literature, Arts and Culture* 1.3 (Spring 2010). Online. Accessed March 29, 2014.

Heffernan, James A. W. *Museum of Words: The Poetics of Ekphrasis from Homer to Ashbery*. Chicago: University of Chicago Press, 1993.

Palladio, Andrea. *The Four Books of Architecture*. Mineola, NY: Dover, 1965.

Verdi, Giuseppe. *Rigoletto, an Opera in Three Acts*. Libretto, Francesco Maria Piave. D. M.'s Opera Site. Online. Accessed March 29, 2014.

Notes

1. Stephen Cheeke. *Writing for Art: The Aesthetics of Ekphrasis* (Manchester, UK: Manchester University Press, 2008), 4.

2. Angie Estes. *Enchantée* (Oberlin: Oberlin College Press, 2013), 17.

3. James A. W. Heffernan. *Museum of Words: The Poetics of Ekphrasis from Homer to Ashbery* (Chicago: University of Chicago Press, 1993), 3.

4. Stephanie Burt. "Nearly Baroque." *The Boston Review* (March/April 2014), 64.

5. Heffernan, 7.

6. Ibid., 7.

7. Umberto Eco. *Art and Beauty in the Middle Ages*, trans. Hugh Bredin (New Haven: Yale University Press, 1986), 54.

8. Estes, *Enchantée*, 17.

9. Dante Alighieri. "Letter to Con Grande," trans. James Marchand. Georgetown University. Online. Accessed March 29, 2014.

10. Angie Estes. *The Uses of Passion* (Salt Lake City: Gibbs Smith, 1995), 54.

11. Ibid., 54.

12. Ibid., 54–55.

13. Ibid., 55.

14. Estes, *Enchantée*, 31.

15. Estes, *The Uses of Passion*, 6.

16. Ibid., 6.
17. Ibid., 7.
18. Angie Estes. *Tryst* (Oberlin: Oberlin College Press, 2009), 7.
19. Ibid., 7.
20. Ibid., 7.
21. Estes, *Enchantée*, 28.
22. Estes, *Tryst*, 53.
23. Ibid., 53.
24. Ibid., 53.
25. Ibid., 54.
26. Ibid., 54–55.
27. Ibid., 55.
28. Giuseppe Verdi. *Rigoletto, an Opera in Three Acts*. Libretto, Francesco Maria Piave. D. M.'s Opera Site. Online. Accessed March 29, 2014, I, i.
29. Estes, *Enchantée*, 55.
30. Ibid., 55.
31. Estes, *Tryst*, 23.
32. Ibid., 24.
33. Angie Estes. *Voice-Over (Oberlin: Oberlin College Press, 2002)*, 11.
34. Angie Estes. *Chez Nous (Oberlin: Oberlin College Press, 2005)*, 4.
35. Ibid., 22–23.
36. Ibid., 36.
37. Ibid., 36.
38. Andrea Palladio. *The Four Books of Architecture* (Mineola, NY: Dover, 1965), 79.
39. Estes, *Chez Nous*, 37.
40. Estes, *Voice-Over*, 7.
41. Ibid., 7.
42. Estes, *Enchantée*, 3.
43. Ibid., 3.

CHRISTOPHER SPAIDE

Ready to Sing
Angie Estes's Enchantée

On its surface, a typical Angie Estes poem is all fun and filigree. But underneath the play—the oxymorons, etymological rabbit holes, multilingual puns—is someone who thinks and feels deeply about her world, largely through European art, broadly defined: visual art, music, and architecture, but also fashion, food, typography. The opening poem of *Chez Nous* (2005), Estes's third book, introduces a speaker whose magnetic attraction to "glamour" can fire off thoughts like a railgun: to the Rita Hayworth film noir quoted in its first lines—"*I can never get a zipper / to close. Maybe that stands / for something, what do you think?*"—or to an equally seductive landscape:

I think glamour is its own
allure, thrashing and
flashing, a lure, a spoon
as in spooning, as in *l'amour*
in Scotland, where I once watched
the gorse-twisted hills unzip
to let a cold blue lake
between them.[1]

In *Enchantée* (2013)—winner of the 2015 Kingsley Tufts Poetry Award—Estes has repurposed her verbal exuberance as a defense against loneliness and loss. These new poems question the purpose and permanence of art, by Estes herself and her predecessors; in several explicitly autobiographical poems, some about her deceased parents, they put Estes on unguarded, unprecedented display. *Enchantée* records a shift in substance that demands a reassessment of style: Estes's established techniques have been forced to adapt to new, troubling subjects.

Polymathic but not pedantic, witty but never at thoughtfulness's expense, conversant with European high art and American kitsch, and blessed with the anagrammatizing mind of a Scrabble prodigy: Estes is someone you'd be *enchantée*, pleased to meet. And she's someone who never quite sounds like anyone else, though like Robyn Schiff and Lucie Brock-Broido (two other allured-to-glamour poets), Estes refuses to stick to any single story, or tone, or genre, for long. Whatever we're calling them—collectors, synthesizers, the attention-deficient aspiring to the condition of poets—Estes, Schiff, and Brock-Broido are poets for whom the question isn't: *what are these poets doing?* It's: *how many things can they do at once?*

What do a fifteenth-century French illuminated manuscript, a Jewish mourning ritual, a gingko tree, breakthroughs of second-century Chinese astronomers, and the deaths of a grandparent and a parent all have in common? Nothing, until arranged into an unsteady constellation in Estes's slender elegy "*Item:*" (the title runs into the poem):

ITEM:

a beautiful hours, very well
and richly illuminated. The yahrzeit candle

beats its yellow heart
all night, and the next morning

the gingko loses all of its leaves
at once. In 185 AD,

Chinese astronomers witnessed
what they called a *guest star*

that appeared in the sky and lingered
for eight months, the first documented

observation of a supernova, death
of a distant star. After his mother

died, my father arrived at her house
to find only a thimble

on the windowsill, erect
as a nipple. And when he

died, I found hanging, dry stone
in his shed, a shrink-wrapped

T-bone steak.[2]

Estes's overstuffed poems can recall unranked lists of the most mar-
velous, though incongruous, items. ("Item," before it became an
English noun, was a Latin adverb meaning "also"; like today's bullet
point, it separated entries on an unranked list.) Her speakers try
their best to wrestle those lists into comprehensibility: in *Enchantée*,
they rarely succeed. The final image of "*Item:*" is a dead body, un-
covered but revealing nothing; where its nipples once were, "where
a pair of // pink doves once blinked," are now two scars like "two
/ eyebrows, raised," expressing a posthumous perplexity.[3]

We recognize Estes by the range of her knowledge, or by her
rapid, restless mind, but also by her bravura wordplay: her lines play
an advanced version of word golf that permits homophones, ana-
grams, mishearings, puns, translations, and etymological backtrack-
ing. Watch what Estes can do with "lips:" "They rustle / like elves
in the leaves, so the French / call them *lèvres*, the levers, lapels / of
the mouth, where we lapse / into ourselves."[4] Other poems play
theme and variations on a single word: in "Afternoon," Estes fits in
the word "slip" eight times, her speech slipping into and out of in-
nuendo: "So let's slip into something more / comfortable, like char-
acter or your native tongue, / and then later, after dinner, we can
slip out / early."[5] But Estes never wanders far from landscapes and
cityscapes, almost always in her adopted continent of Europe. And
she is enamored with quotables and trivia, culled from science, lex-
icography, anthropology, celebrity culture, history, and (increasingly
in *Enchantée*) her own personal history.

The centerpiece of an Estes poem, though, is her breathless ap-
preciation of art. Dropping allusions as she goes, a single Estes
poem illuminates every artwork by the light of a dozen others, no
matter their distances in space, time, or medium. "*Hail to Thee,*"
(again, the title runs into the poem) lifts its title from Shelley's "To
a Skylark," but within a few lines it bounds from skylark to soup, a
chef's prep work to Walter Benjamin's *Passagenwerk*:

I write, my wrist nodding
　　　　as it does when chopping leeks
　　and garlic with a knife, then stirring
the soup, whose project—with farro,
　　　　ceci, and nettles—is *to present life*
　　as it has been forgotten.[6]

The artistic virtue Estes admires most she calls the "Baroque." Her earlier poem *"Rendez-Vous"* paid tribute to Bernini's sculpture *Ecstasy of Saint Teresa*, by way of comparison to *"pâtisserie,"* flowers, and a musical *"appoggiatura."*[7] And her wordplay echoes some of the Baroque era's serious trifles, like Bach's inscription of the four-note motif B-A-C-H, not only as an in-joke for future musicologists but as a crucial scaffolding for his compositions.

In Estes's usage, though, "Baroque" stretches out to encompass art from before the capital-B Baroque era—illuminated manuscripts, medieval painting, iconography—and art much later—Miles Davis and John Coltrane, midcentury film, contemporary art. Her Baroque refers to anything, from any era, that wears extravagant ornament for extravagant ornament's sake. In the earlier poem *"Sans Serif,"* Estes rejects the titular font for appearing "clean / and spare, like Cassius it has that lean / and hungry look." Its central declaration reads as both haughty send-off and personal manifesto: "It's the opposite of / Baroque, so I want / none of it." Estes's Baroque isn't the least bit weighed down by the baggage of serifs or "a lick / of gold leaf," a soprano's *appoggiatura* or the icing on the (here, literal) cake. Apparent add-ons, to her mind, are indispensable, both to the otherwise "lean / and hungry" lives we lead and to the opulent art that decorates and describes them.[8]

Though the Baroque snakes through all of Estes's poems, twisting them into asymmetrical and exquisite shapes, *Enchantée* is her first collection to envision the Baroque's possible failure. "Ars Poetica" conjures the Baroque in hallucinatory form, only to witness its downfall:

　　I once dreamed a word entirely
　　Baroque: a serpentine line of letters leaning
　　with the flourish of each touching the shoulder
　　of another so that one breath at the word's
　　beginning made them all collapse.[9]

Earlier poems charmed with the notion that the Baroque could sustain perpetual motion and impeccable form: every letter would lean on another, each flourish give way to flourish. *Enchantée* is not so naïve: its sorrowful songs of experience recognize that the intake of "one breath" can spell not only the collapse of a dream "entirely / Baroque" but the end of a life. Estes's new poems are still repositories of curiosities, but their trivia tends toward the morbid, toward instructions like "How to Know When the Dead Are Dead":

> To be sure the dead are dead,
> Greeks would cut off a finger, Slavs rubbed bodies
>
> with warm water for an hour, while Hebrews wait
> for putrefaction because even without hands, the dove
> still plays her flute.[10]

Enchanted as ever by art, now Estes finds herself drawn to representations of the dead: the body of Christ, Leonardo da Vinci's meditations on corpses, Dante's imaginative afterlife. Even Estes's wordplay, her poems' most reliable source of fun, hints at alienation, dislocations of time and space, endings of all kinds. Puns have turned painful—"*Pietà*" opens: "It was the end / of an era, the end of / *to be.*" "*Era*" in Italian means not only "age" or "period" but also "she was" or "he was"; in these poems, where multilingualism is the baseline, "the end of an era" transforms from cliché to elegy: he was, she was, no more.[11] Other word games address lonesomeness in the living: "Cache," a poem set in the "hectic site" of Paris's Île de la Cité, speaks three languages in as many terse lines: "yesterday, / here, *hier* and *ici*, the icy ache / of *ich*." Simply by translating some words and spelling out others—"*hier*" (almost a homophone of "here") and "*ici*" are French for "yesterday" and "here," while "icy ache" sounds out the letters of "*ich*," German's first-person pronoun—Estes conjures a lonely, aching "I," a solo voice drowned out by a cacophony of languages.[12]

"Cache" is one among many poems in *Enchantée* to close with tortuous, tragicomic wordplay, and with its restless lines and zippering indentation, one among many to signal Estes's increasing experimentation with form. Where earlier poems, "True Confessions" and "*Sans Serif*" included, arrived in an unbroken streak of two-to-four-beat, left-margin-aligned lines, Estes now varies line-lengths and white space to mirror feelings too unruly for that clipped, quippy standard. *Enchantée* changes forms *between* every poem, forms *for* every poem: for the decomposing relationship of "*Brief Encounter*" (after David Lean's 1945 film), Estes writes spaced-out, wrenched-open couplets, with no two neighboring lines perfectly flush:

> The story is *the only one*
> > > *I can tell and the only one I can*
>
> > > *never tell*, she says after she has left
> her lover for the last time, in voiceover
>
> to her husband, *the only one I can tell*
> > *and the only one I can never*
>
> > *tell.*[13]

Like the lovers of the poem and the film, these coupled lines can never quite agree. Estes also writes page-spanning, sparsely punctuated poems; poems portioned into drastically dissimilar sections; poems in ad hoc shaped stanzas; and several poems written in tercets, suffused with Italian culture, close to but never perfectly replicating *terza rima*.

Doubtless, the *Divine Comedy* has inspired some of Estes's new forms, but the influence does not stop there: Dante appears in (by my count) twelve of the book's thirty-one poems. (Her passion for art is tempered by an academic's remove—she includes scholarly references in the back of every book; her poems helpfully translate most foreign phrases, and enter or exit their allusions with clear markers: "Mallarmé said . . . ." "According to Leonardo. . . ." "In *Purgatory*. . . .") Estes admires Dante in part for his irreverent, intrepid approach to language, for going where no Italian has gone before: "Evening" travels back to childhood and across the Milky Way but turns on Dante's coinage of the verb "*dislagarsi*," to "unlake itself."[14] More important, in Estes's austere elegies, Dante recurs as a model artist who can imaginatively represent what happens to us after death in ways that are always beautiful, rarely true.

Hence *Enchantée*'s core paradox: its Dantean poems are simultaneously its most autobiographical; revisiting Estes's childhood and personal life, they send us seven centuries back and a continent away. In a practice that recalls allegorical interpretation of scripture, Estes superimposes past onto present, Dante's Europe onto her

America, canonical literature onto autobiography. In a 2010 interview, Estes explains that she'd been "doing a kind of medieval 'anagogical' thinking most of life—reading the details of this world in the light of some other world."[15] As "Evening," adapting *Paradiso* IX:108, wishfully describes, a God like Dante's "makes the world above / inform the world below."[16]

These superimpositions animate one of *Enchantée*'s most astonishing poems, "Shadow of the Evening." The poem describes, and analogizes, three figures: first, a bronze Etruscan statue, "22" tall by 4" wide," known as *L'Ombra della sera* (the shadow of the evening); second, an incorporeal "shade" out of Dante; third, Estes's own brother. The poem's first half recounts, in familiar Baroque style, the statue's origins; its second half hurtles abruptly into a personal episode, returning to

> . . . that evening
> in 1949 when my brother—he must have been
> three—crawled over the front seat
> of the car towards the back, reached for
> the push-down handle of the door and
> fell out, rolling down the road as my parents
> sped by. My mother turned to grasp him
> the way Dante keeps trying
> to clasp a shade, wrapping her arms
> around her own chest.[17]

Estes is rarely so narrative, so generous with autobiographical details, as she is here. In that same 2010 interview, she calls herself "uneasy with 'personal' detail and 'narrative thread' . . . because of their tendency to claim some 'authentic' realm of experience that doesn't feel to me to be the experience the poem is really enacting or giving rise to."[18] Unlike many verse-autobiographers, Estes prefers lyric to narrative, artificial to "authentic." Triangulating her brother with two artificial figures—the shadow-thin statue and the insubstantial "shade," all of them impossible to grasp firmly—Estes makes her experiences somehow more of a piece, somehow more intelligible, even if by a self-conscious act of contrivance.

For every poem layering art onto life, making sense of one through the other, *Enchantée* offers a poem that casts art into unforgiving doubt, unheard of in Estes's work until now. Sometimes, taking Platonist cues, she depicts art as a copy of a copy of a copy: "Note" displays "the photograph of my mother's great / grandfa-

ther printed from a negative made / from a photograph of a nega-
tive, which we / Xeroxed for keeps."[19] In starkly anti-Baroque fash-
ion, these verbal repetitions offer no advancement, no embellishment.
In contrast, "*I Want to Talk About You*" worries that art is only embel-
lishment, just outward show: Estes's long, breathless lines compare
the flight of starlings to "a woolen scarf wrapping // and wrapping,
nothing at the center but throat" and to "extended cadenzas to
pieces that // never get played."[20] Estes's qualms rarely resolve
neatly, but in her last poem, she concludes that these are all moot
questions—we will keep making and appreciating art, no matter
what. The drive to create is inborn, involuntary, inescapable: her
book's final five lines, quoting from Gaston Bachelard's *The Poetics
of Space*, leave us with one last anecdote.

> Bachelard recalls how
>   the French baritone said it is impossible
>
> to think the vowel sound *ah* without
>   tensing, tightening the vocal chords: *we read* ah
>   *and the voice is ready to sing.*[21]

Any one Estes poem gives the impression of doing everything at
once, but a whole book may leave some readers feeling, or fearing,
that this transcription of our world leaves out a lot: race, any social
gathering of three or more people, modern technology (save for a
lone iPad in "Almost Autumn"), most current events, the less-than-
Baroque arts, and pretty much anything that has ever happened
outside of Western Europe, the United States, and one or two parts
of Asia. Certain readers may shy from Estes for the same reasons
they avoid James Merrill, or Wes Anderson, and their cloistered,
Europhilic, aesthetic (as in "aesthete") sensibilities.

But if any living poet could convince us that art and life share
the same high stakes and same high style, that the Baroque is life at
its most bracing and best, it's Estes. *Enchantée* makes her case in su-
perlative ways—it's her most Dantean book, her most experimental,
her most mournful, her most serious (and least purely fun, perhaps).
For new readers, it offers the best introduction to Estes to date. In
retrospect, *Enchantée*'s primary subject—not art, not language, not
the Baroque, but what any of the three can or can't do to make our
lives any different—was her hidden subject all along. In *Enchantée*,

Estes has fashioned that familiar question into memorable, musical forms: with her exuberant poems, she has given us good answers.

Notes

1. Angie Estes. *Chez Nous* (Oberlin: Oberlin College Press, 2005), 1.
2. Angie Estes. *Enchantée* (Oberlin: Oberlin College Press, 2013), 39.
3. Ibid., 40.
4. Ibid., 60–61.
5. Ibid., 20.
6. Ibid., 49.
7. Estes, *Chez Nous*, 4.
8. Ibid., 28.
9. Estes, *Enchantée*, 56.
10. Ibid., 41.
11. Ibid., 16.
12. Ibid., 8.
13. Ibid., 18.
14. Ibid., 34.
15. Karen Rigby. "Means of Transport, Medieval Mind: Dialogue with Angie Estes." *See above page 68.*
16. Estes, *Enchantée*, 34.
17. Ibid., 57.
18. Rigby, "Means of Transport," p. 72.
19. Estes, *Enchantée*, 26–27.
20. Ibid., 5.
21. Ibid., 64.

Contributors

Julianne Buchsbaum's three collections of poetry are *Slowly, Slowly, A Little Night Comes*, and *The Apothecary's Heir*. Her work has appeared in *Verse, Southwest Review*, and *Harvard Review*, among other publications. She lives and works in Lawrence, Kansas, where she is a humanities librarian for the University of Kansas.

Kevin Clark is the author of two volumes of poems, *Self-Portrait with Expletives* (2008) and *In the Evening of No Warning* (2002), and a creative writing textbook, *The Mind's Eye: A Guide to Writing Poetry*. Clark's writing appears in such places as *Crazyhorse, Ploughshares*, and the *Georgia, Iowa*, and *Southern* reviews.

Leah Falk's poems and essays have appeared in *Kenyon Review, FIELD, 32 Poems, Blackbird, Los Angeles Review of Books*, and elsewhere. She works at the Writers House at Rutgers University–Camden.

B. K. Fischer is the author of three books of poetry—*Mutiny Gallery, St. Rage's Vault*, and the forthcoming *My Lover's Discourse*—and a critical study, *Museum Mediations: Reframing Ekphrasis in Contemporary American Poetry*. She teaches at Columbia University and is a poetry editor at *Boston Review*.

Langdon Hammer is poetry editor of *The American Scholar* and Chair of the Department of English at Yale. He is the author of *Hart Crane and Allen Tate: Janus-Faced Modernism* and editor of *O My Land, My Friends: The Selected Letters of Hart Crane* and *Hart Crane: Complete Poems and Selected Letters*, and is currently at work on a biography of James Merrill.

Mark Irwin is the author of nine collections of poetry, including *A Passion According to Green* (2017), *Tall If* (2008), and *Bright Hunger* (2004), as well as a collection of essays, *Monster: Distortion, Abstrac-*

tion, and Originality in Contemporary American Poetry (2017). He teaches in the Creative Writing & Literature PhD Program at the University of Southern California.

Nancy Kuhl is Curator of Poetry for the Yale Collection of American Literature at the Beinecke Rare Book and Manuscript Library at Yale University. She is author of the poetry collections *The Wife of the Left Hand* (2007) and *Suspend* (2010), as well as the chapbooks *In the Arbor* (1997) and *The Nocturnal Factory* (2008).

Karen Rigby is the author of *Chinoiserie* (2012) and two chapbooks, *Savage Machinery* (2008) and *Festival Bone* (2004). Her work has appeared in *FIELD, jubilat, Black Warrior Review, Southern Indiana Review*, and other journals. She lives in Arizona.

Jill Allyn Rosser has written four collections of poems, most recently *Mimi's Trapeze* (2014). She is Professor of English at Ohio University, where she has also served as editor of *New Ohio Review*.

Doug Rutledge is the editor of *Ceremony and Text in the Renaissance* and the author, with photographer Abdi Roble, of *The Somali Diaspora: A Journey Away*. His poetry and reviews have appeared in numerous journals, including *Chautauqua Literary Journal, Southern Humanities Review*, and Harvard Review, online.

Christopher Spaide is a PhD candidate at Harvard University. His reviews have appeared in *Boston Review, The New Yorker* online, *Slate*, and *Yale Review*. His poetry has appeared in *The Common* and *Poetry*.

Lee Upton is the author of fourteen books, including six poetry collections, four books of literary criticism, and a short story collection, *The Tao of Humiliation* (2014). She is Francis A. March Professor of English and Writer-in-Residence at Lafayette College.

Ahren Warner is poetry editor of *Poetry London*. He is the author of two collections of poetry—*Confer* (2011) and *Pretty* (2013)—and is working on a third, *Hello. Your Promise Has Been Extracted*. Warner lives in Paris.

David Young is the author of volumes of poetry including *Field of Light and Shadow: Selected and New Poems* and *Seasoning: A Poet's Year*, several books on Shakespeare; and translations of Rilke, Miroslav Holub, Petrarch, Du Fu, and Basho. He works as an editor at Oberlin College Press.

Printed and bound by CPI Group (UK) Ltd, Croydon, CR0 4YY

09/06/2025

14685638-0001